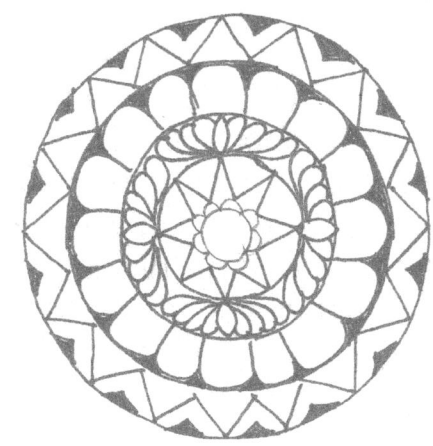

"MIND"ala

By

Karry Weather

Printed in 2017
Text, images and photographs produced by Karry Weather.

No part of this publication may be reproduced or transmitted in any form whatsoever without prior permission obtained in writing.

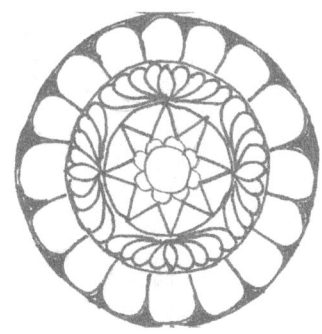
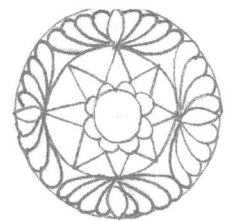

"MIND"ala is a colouring experience for adults new to colouring as well as more experienced practitioners. All the pictures allow adults to enjoy shading and intricate colouring whilst exploring mindfulness and enjoying that special moment. It is a book that can be enjoyed individually or by the whole family, allowing younger members to experience the pleasure of successful and controlled colouring.

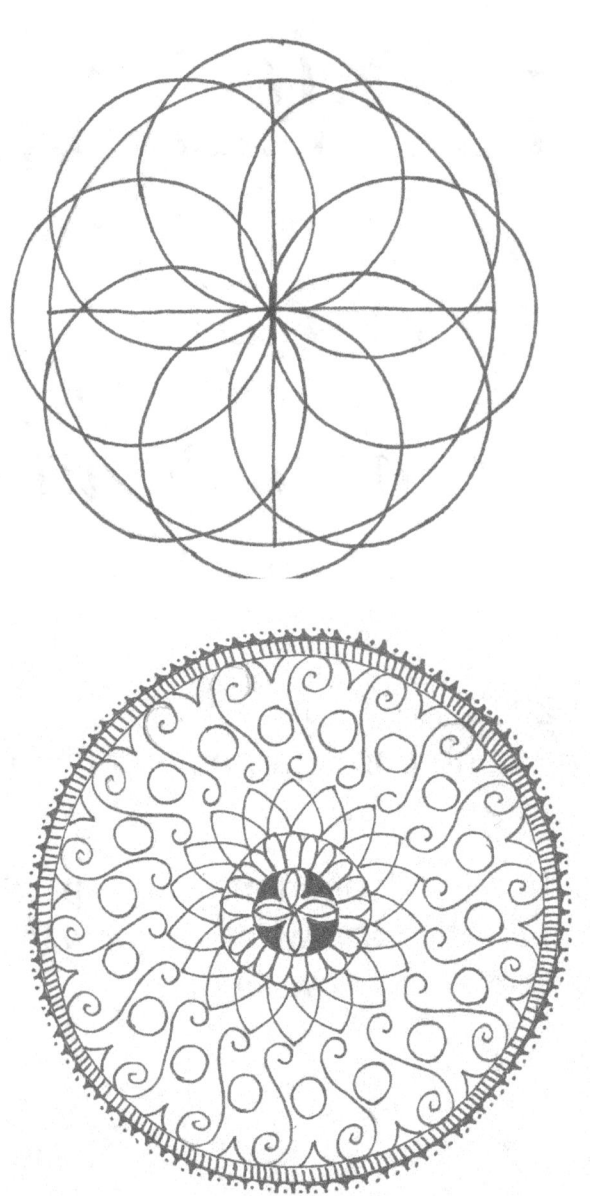

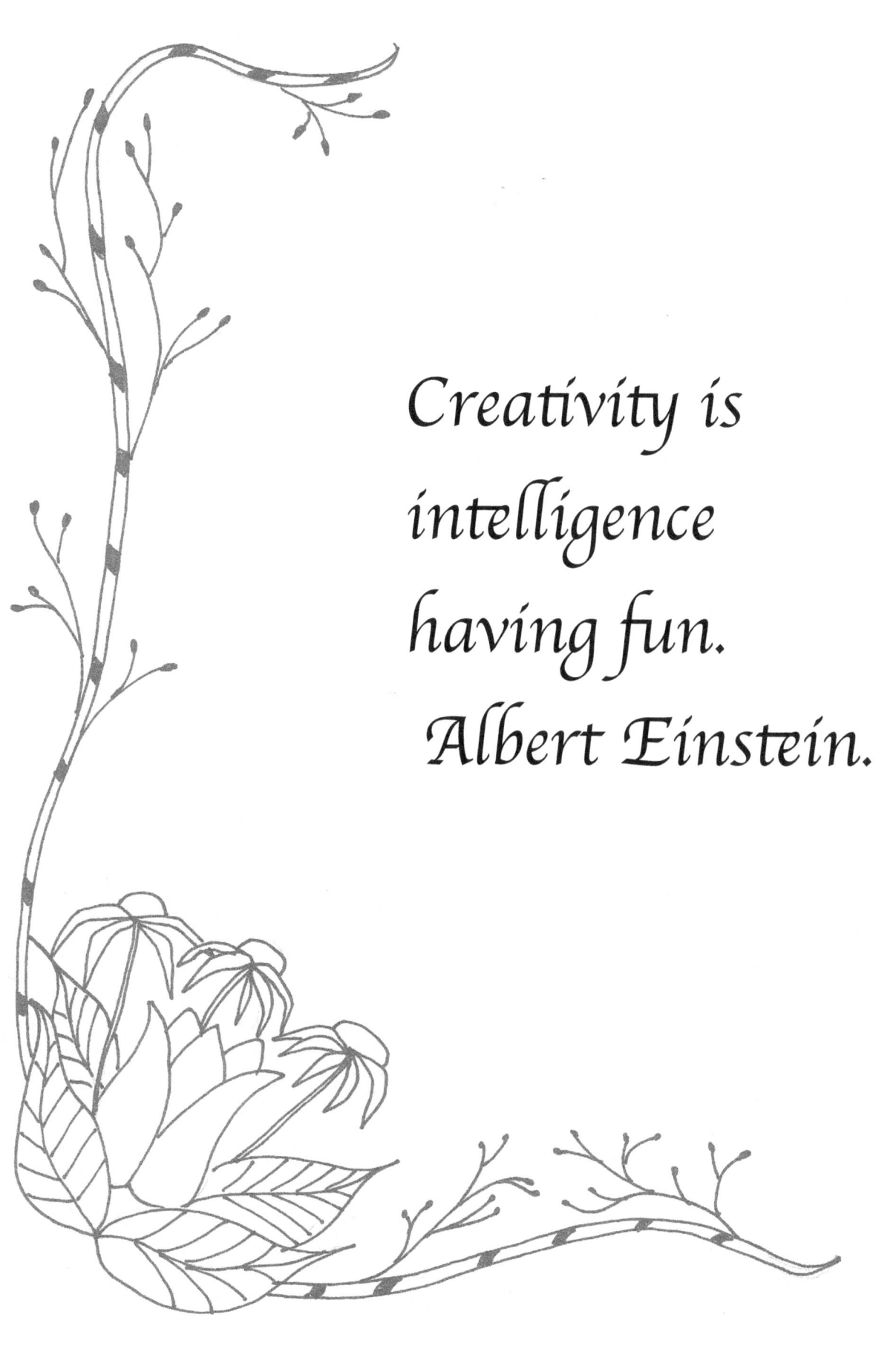

Creativity is intelligence having fun.
Albert Einstein.

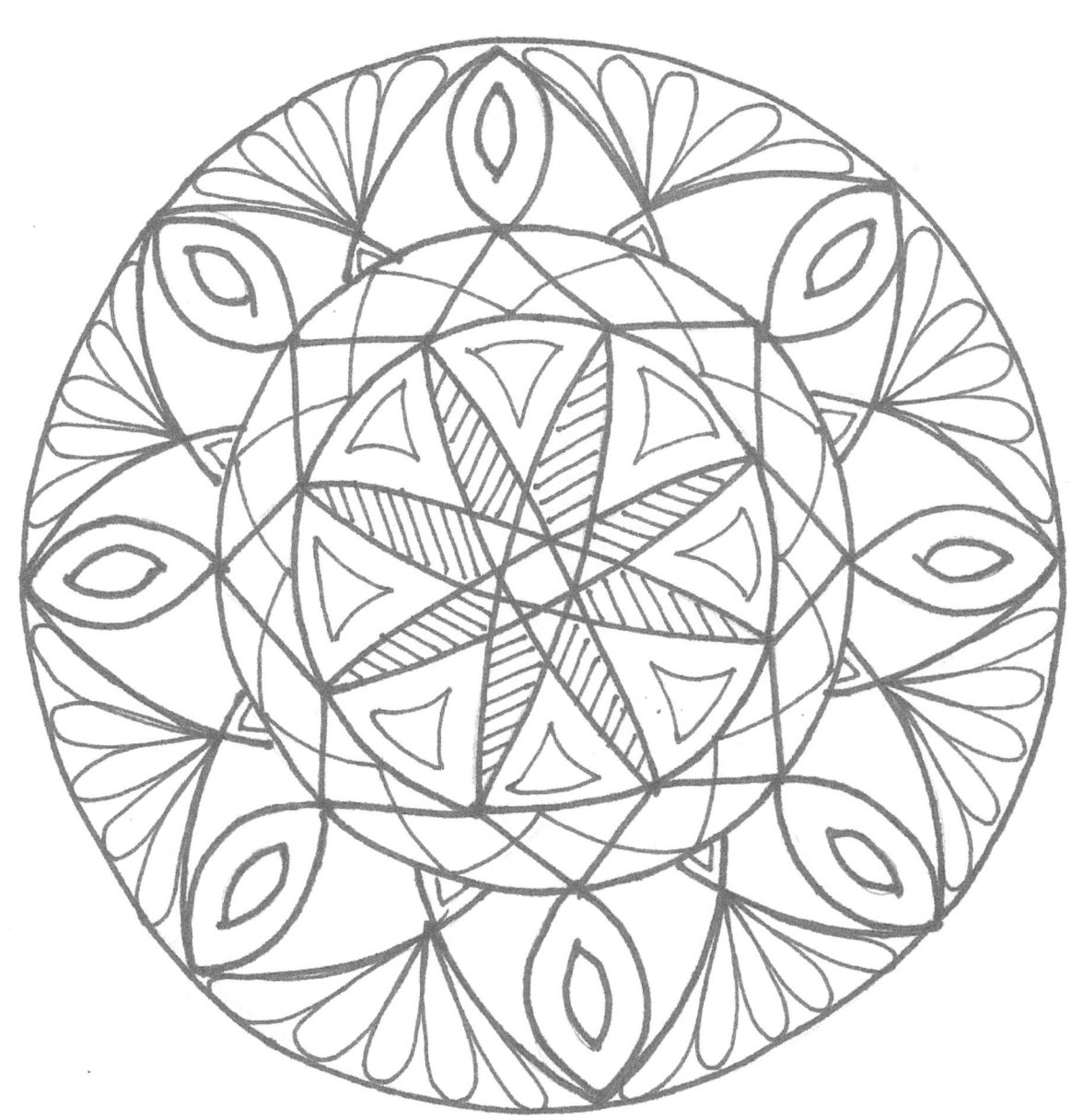

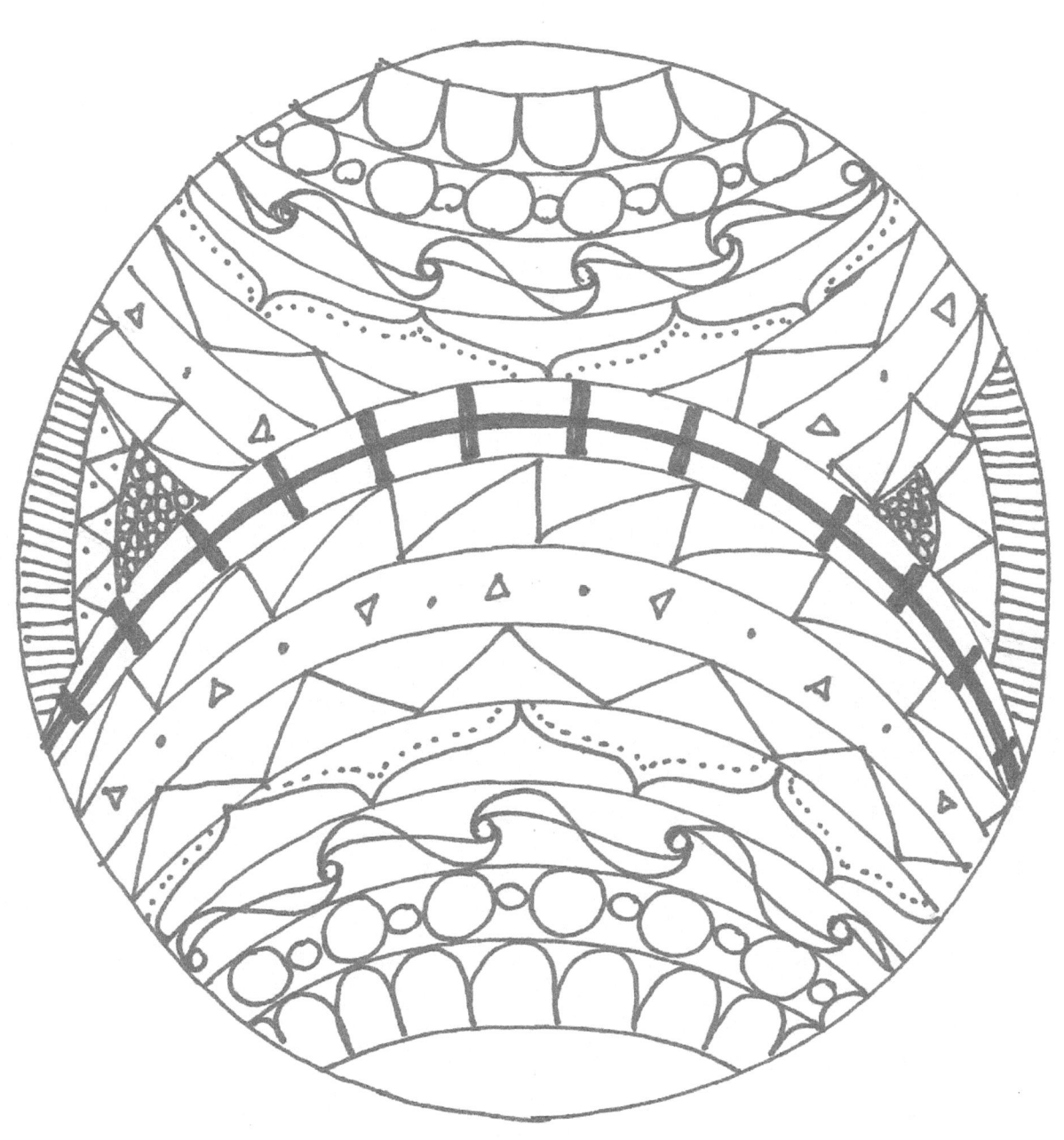

Colour me happy.

Anon

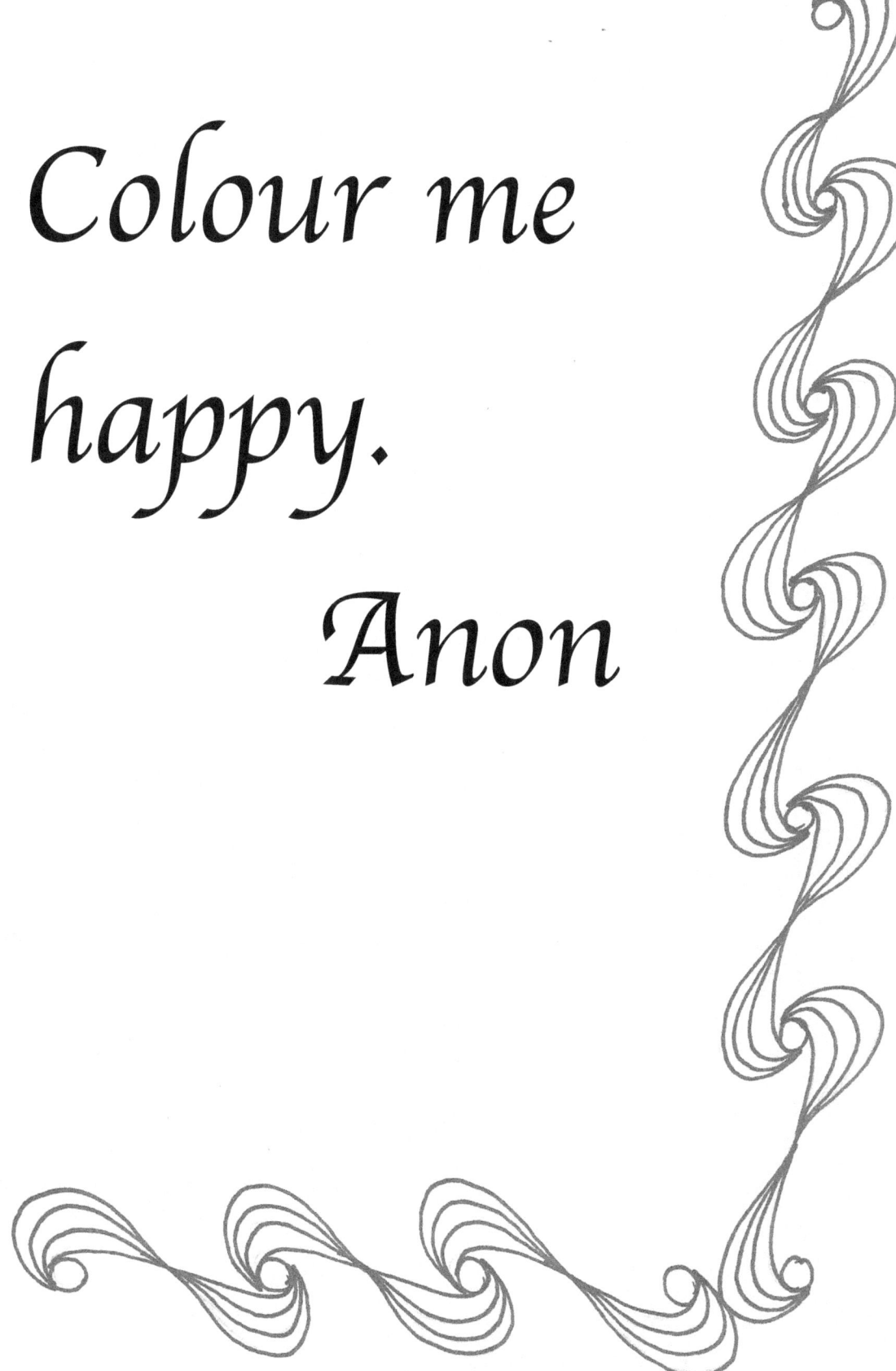

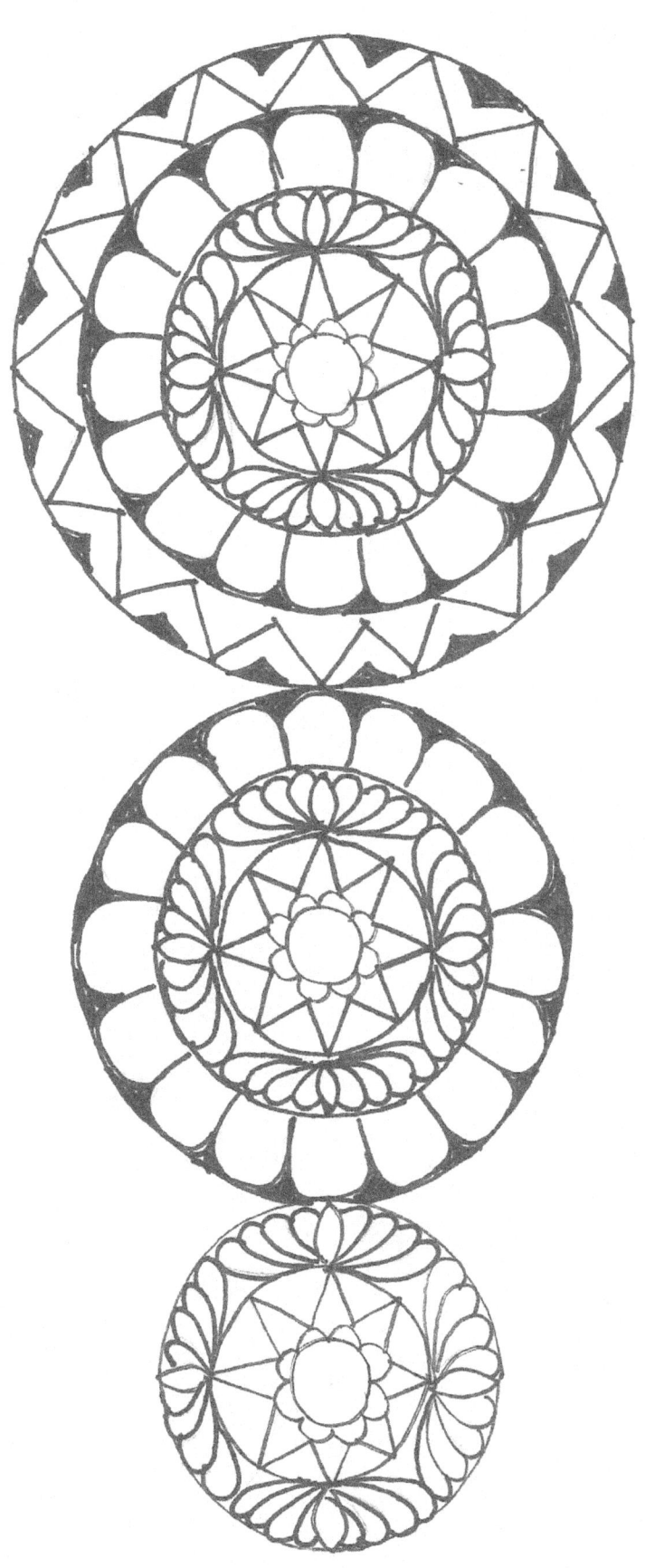

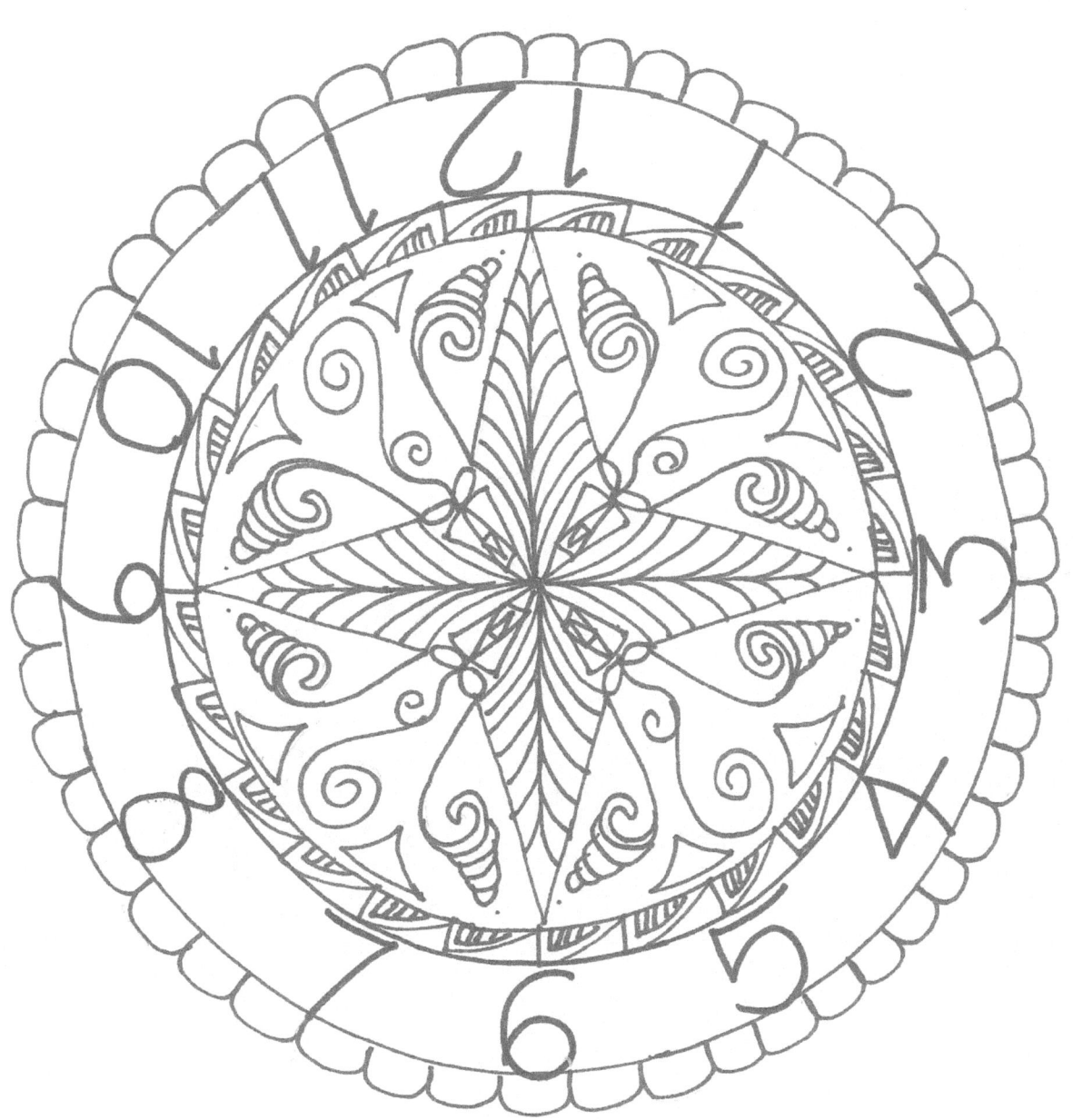

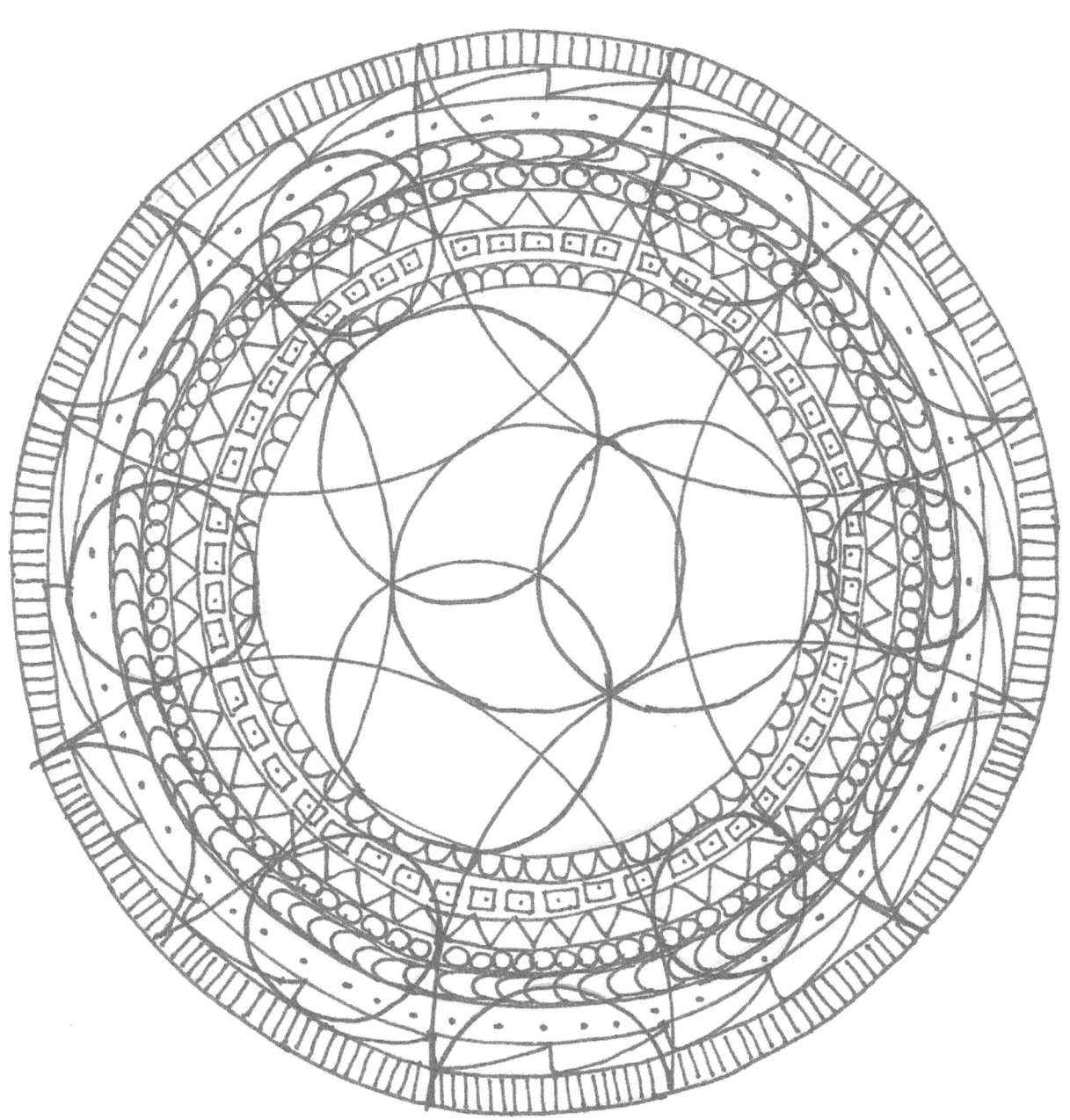

Life doesn't require that we be the best, only that we try our best.

H. Jackson Brown jnr.

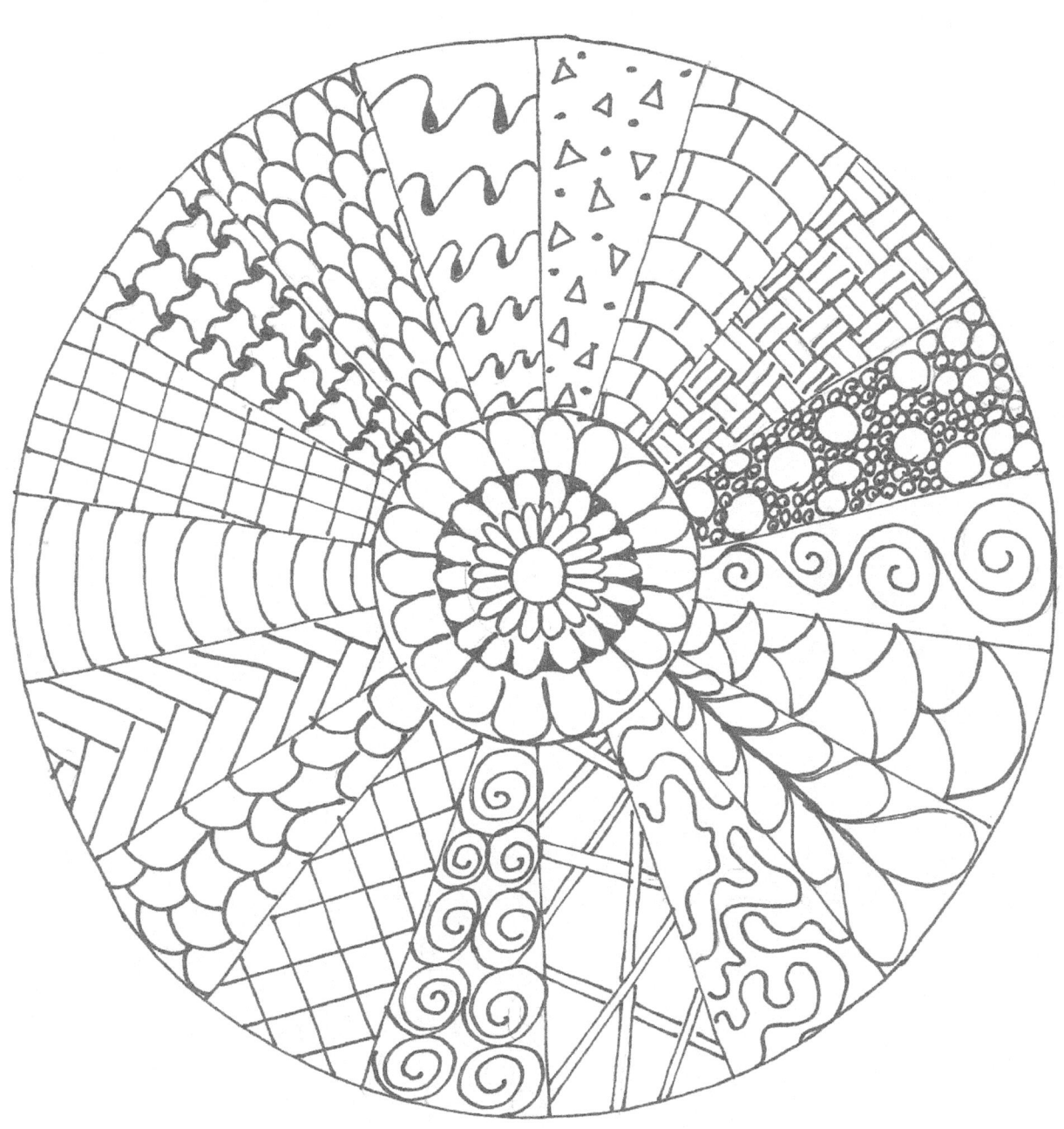

If you want to fly, give up everything that weighs you down.
  Anon

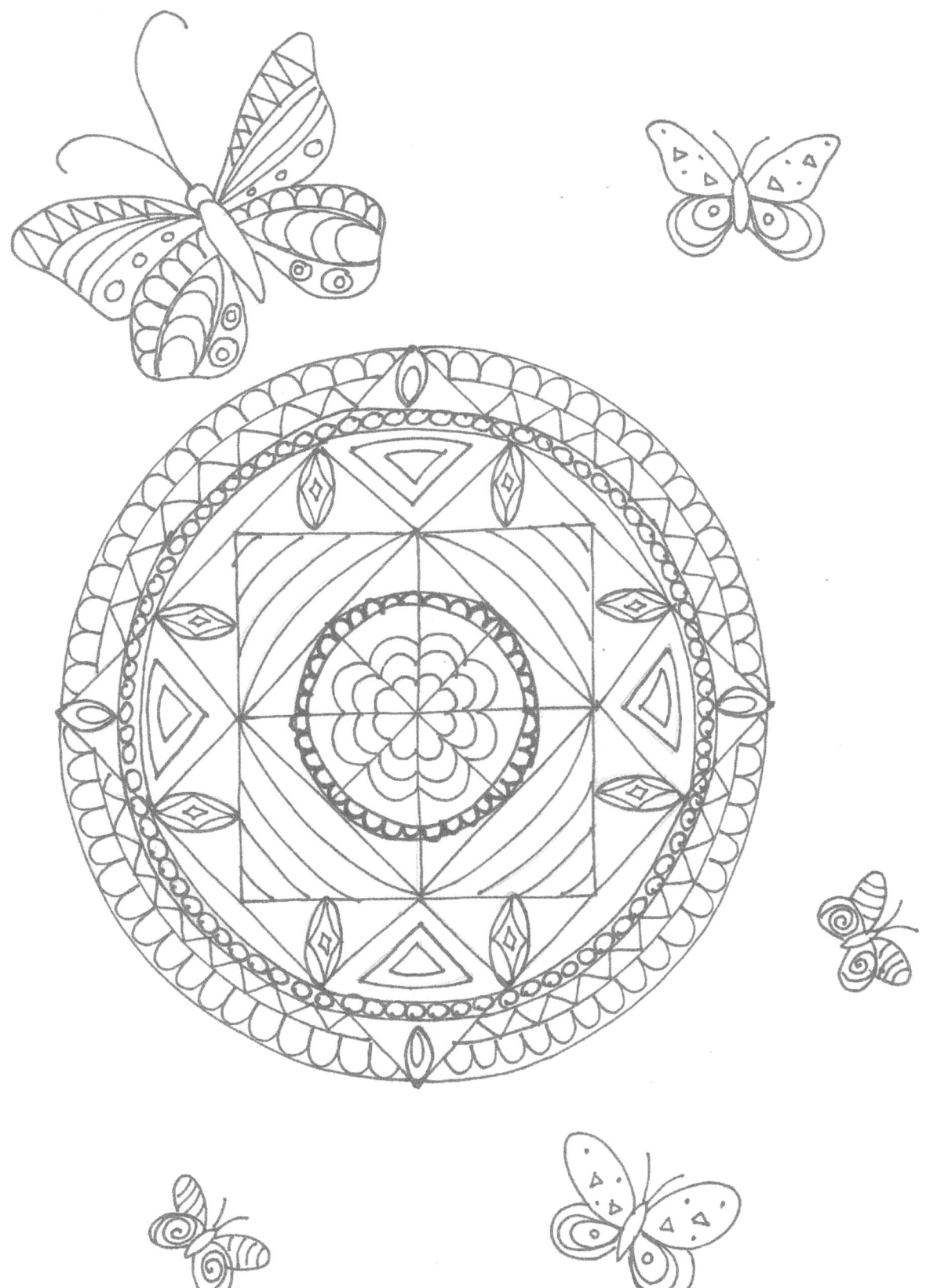

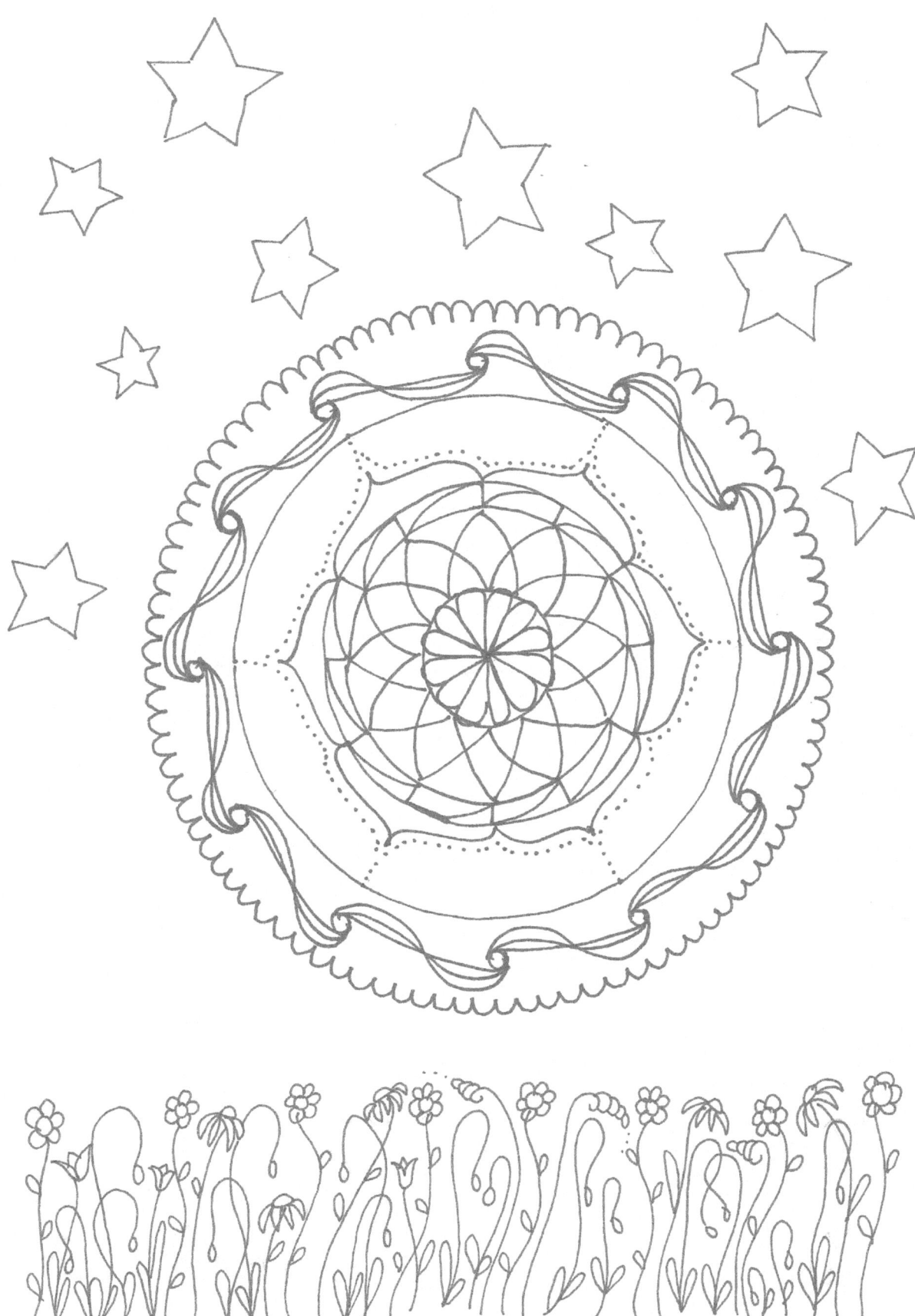

Do life your own way.
Anon.

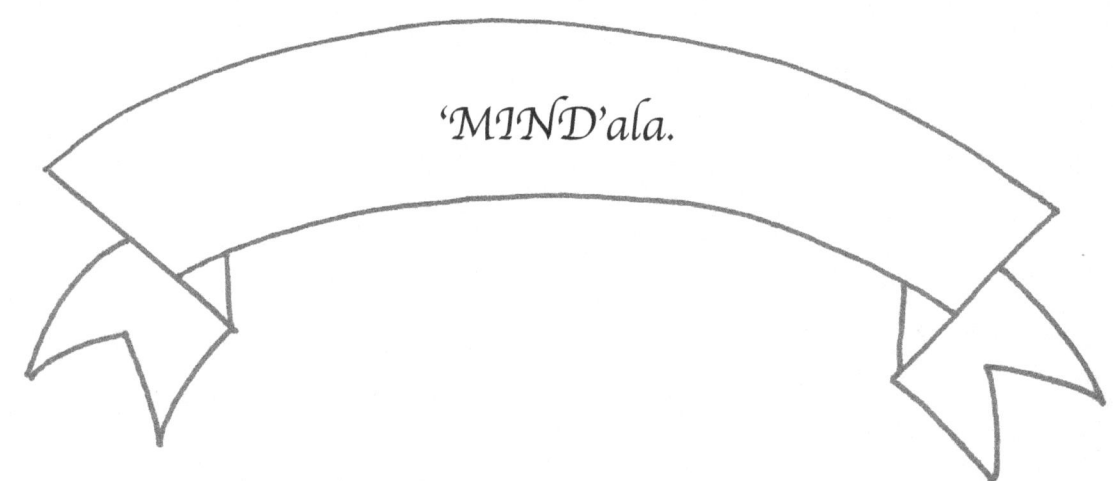

'MIND'ala.

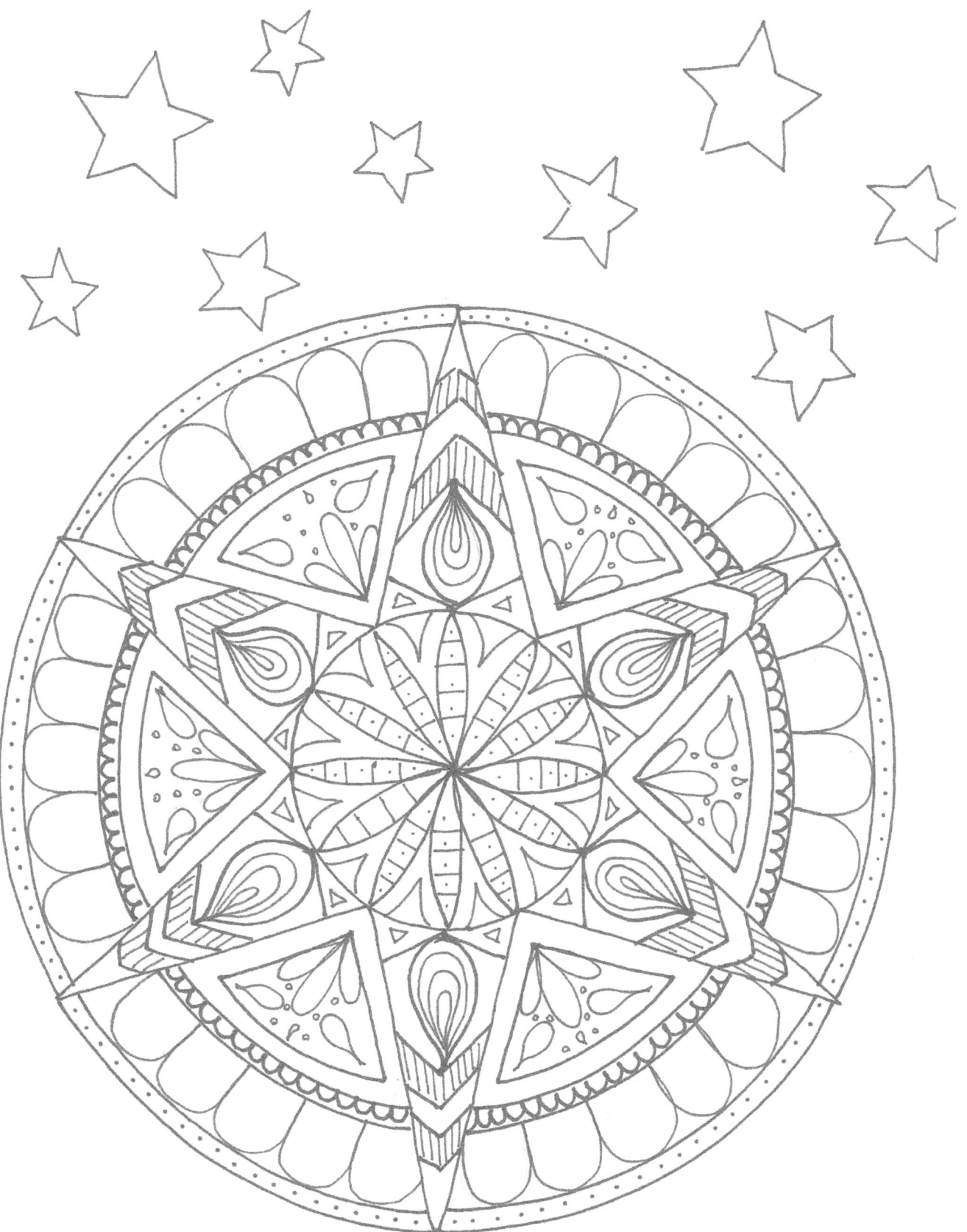

When it rains look for rainbows, when it is dark look for stars.

                    Anon.

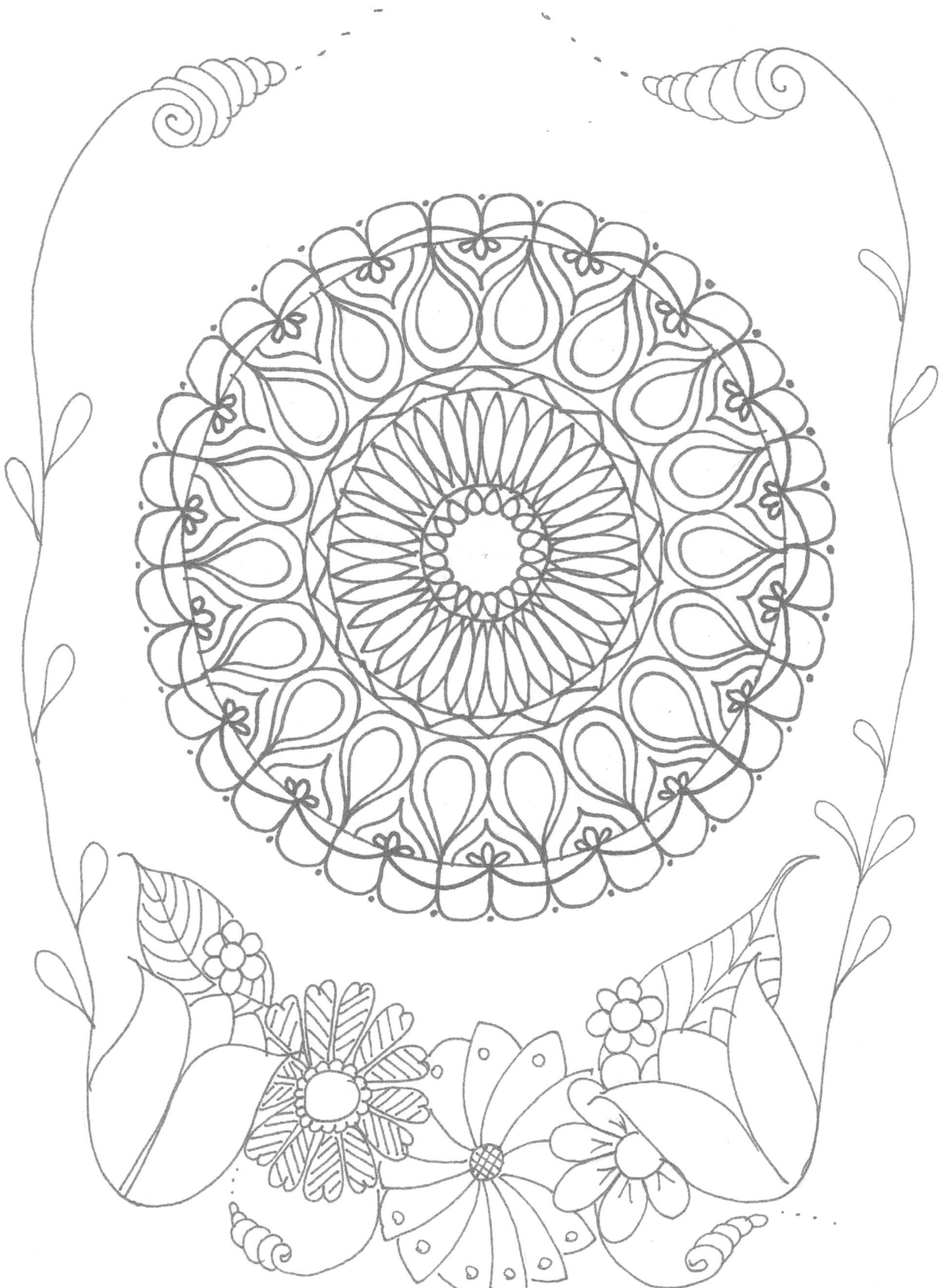

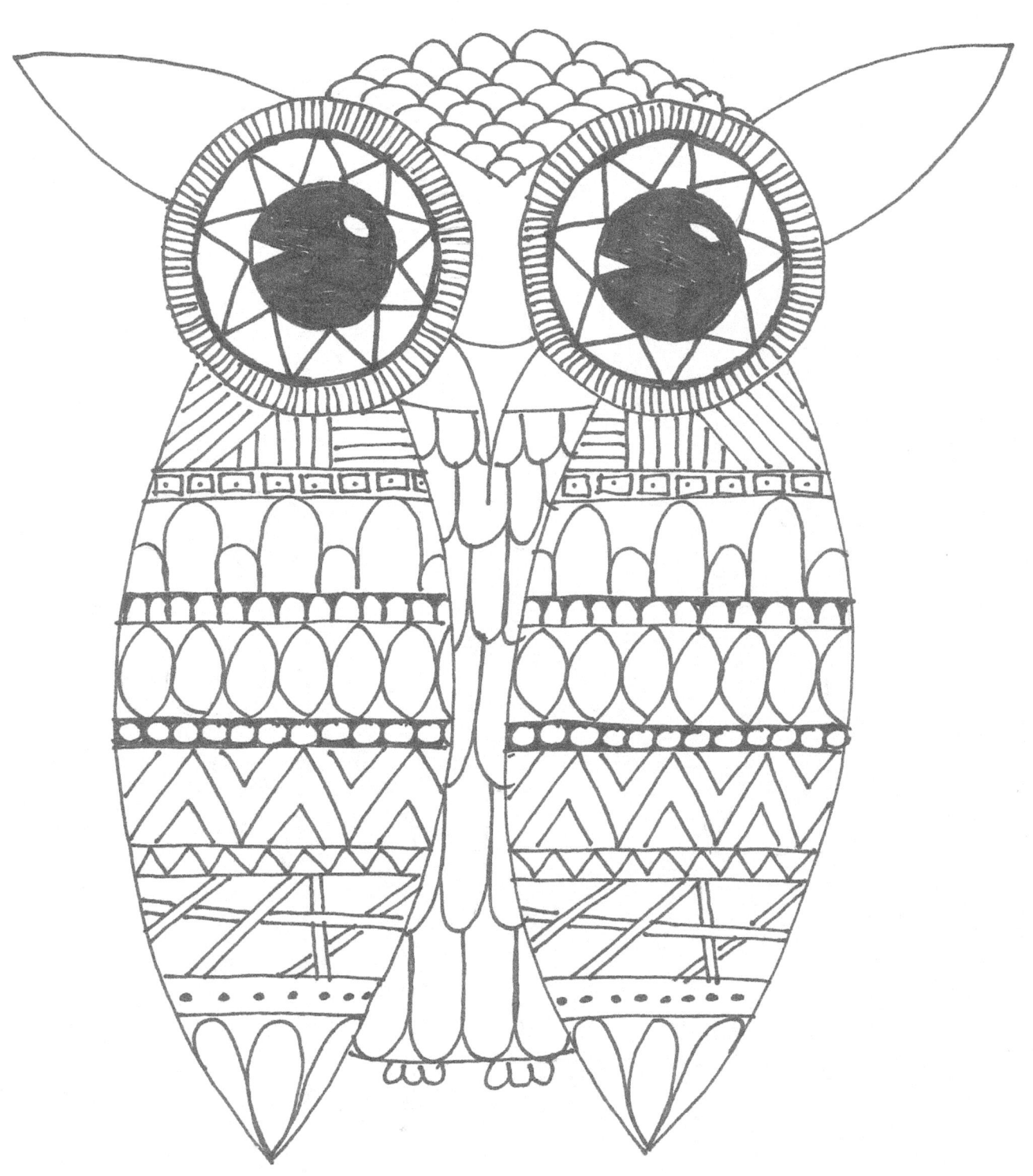

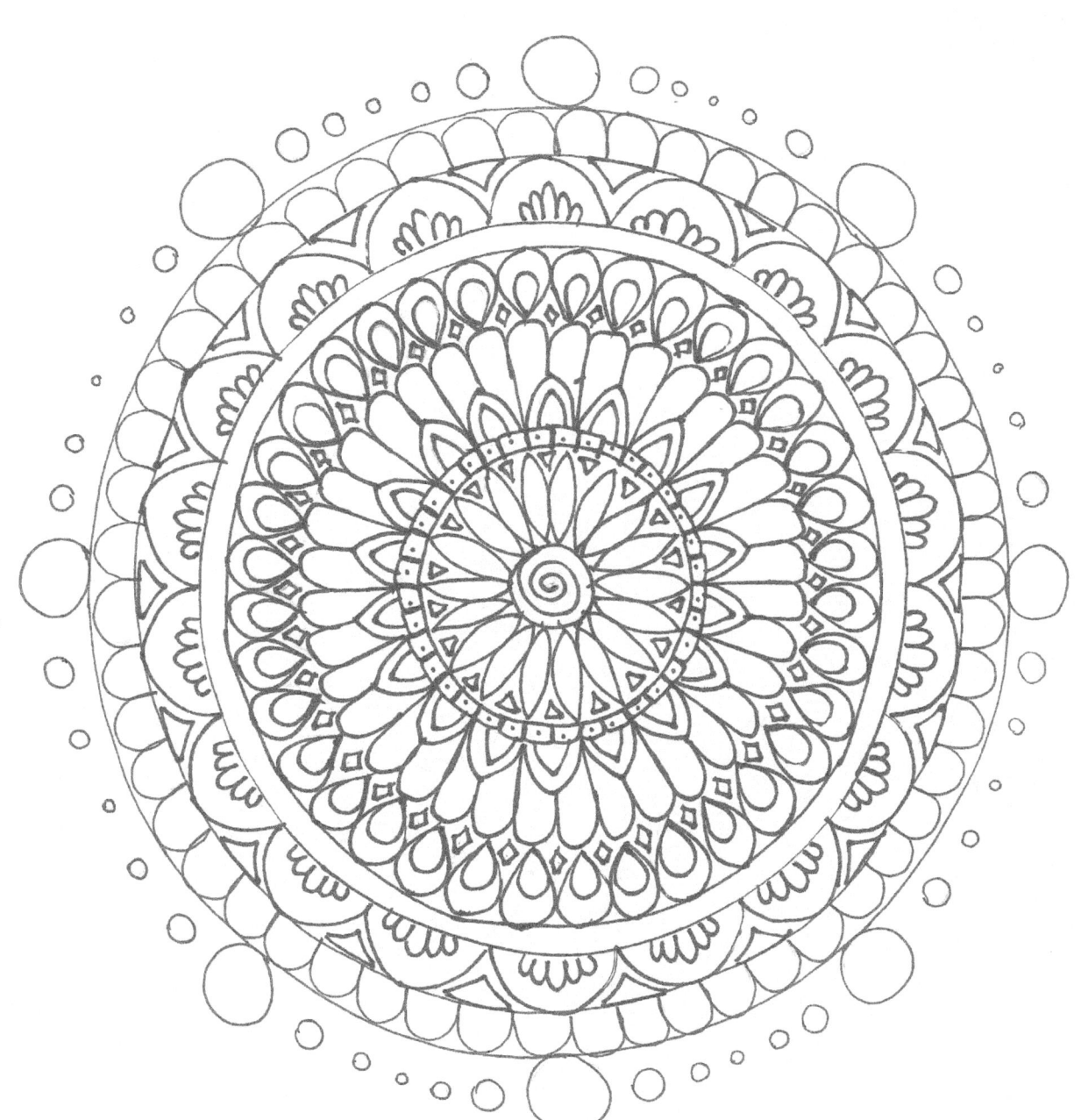

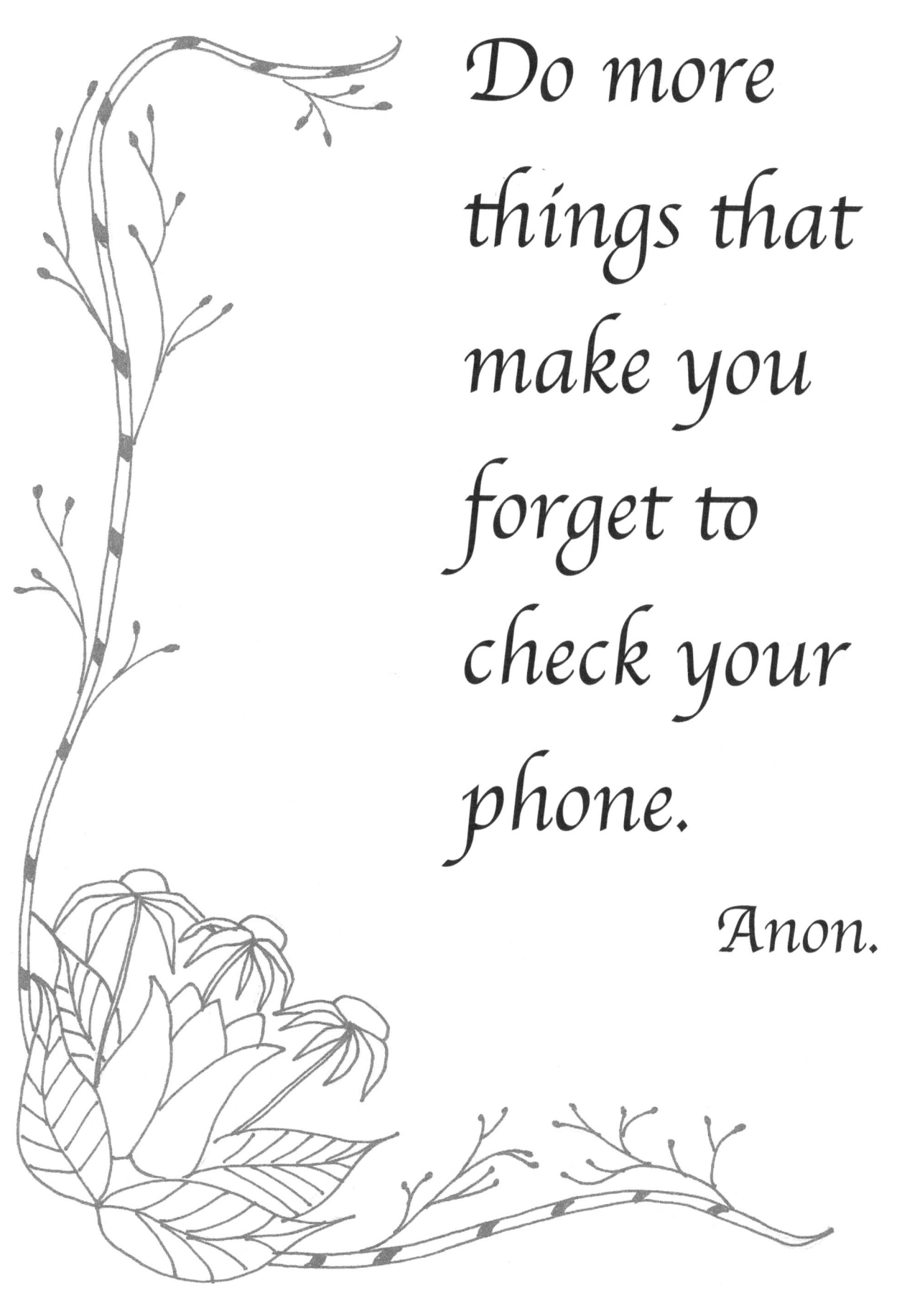

Do more things that make you forget to check your phone.

Anon.

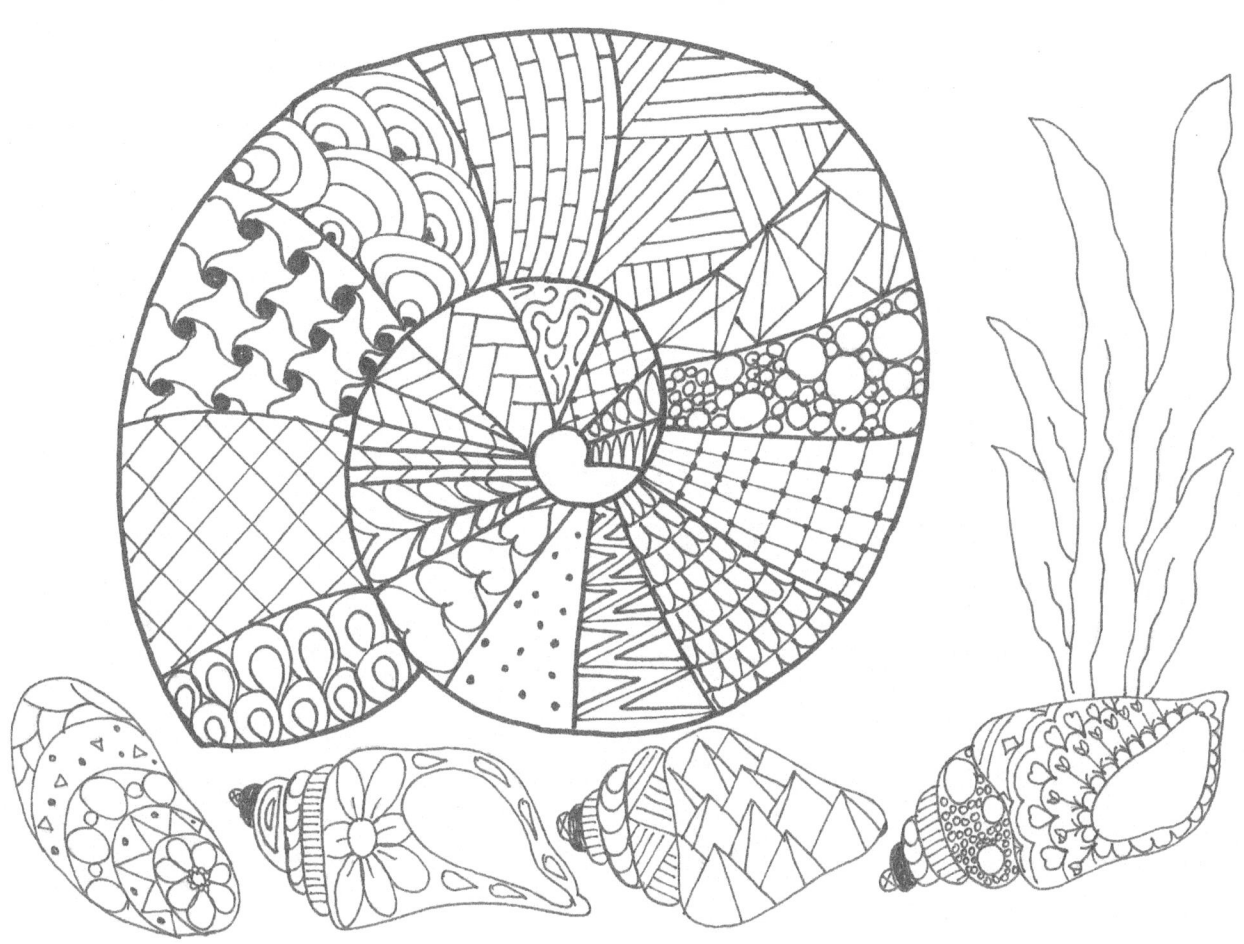

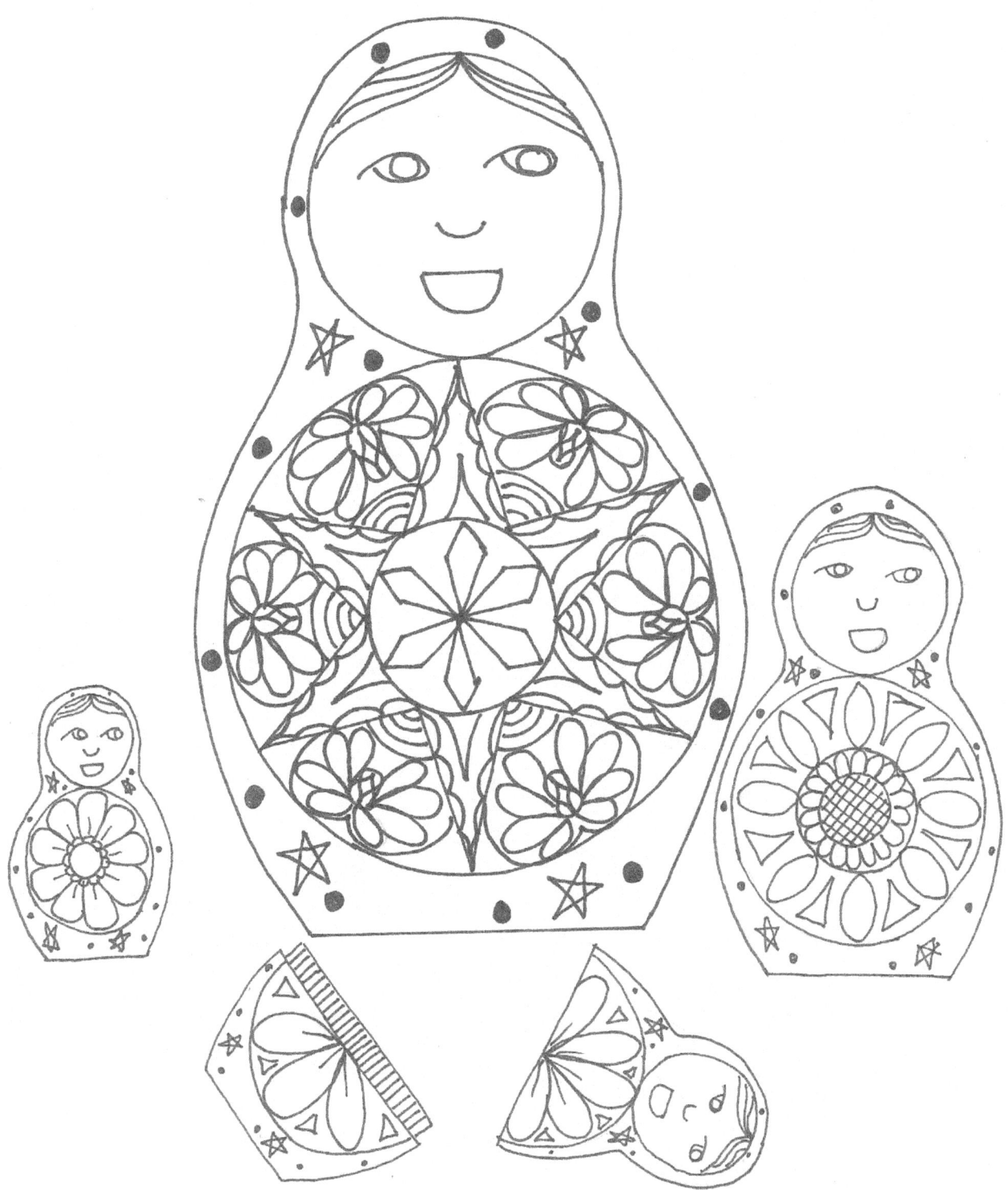

No act of
kindness,
however small,
is ever wasted.

    Aesop.

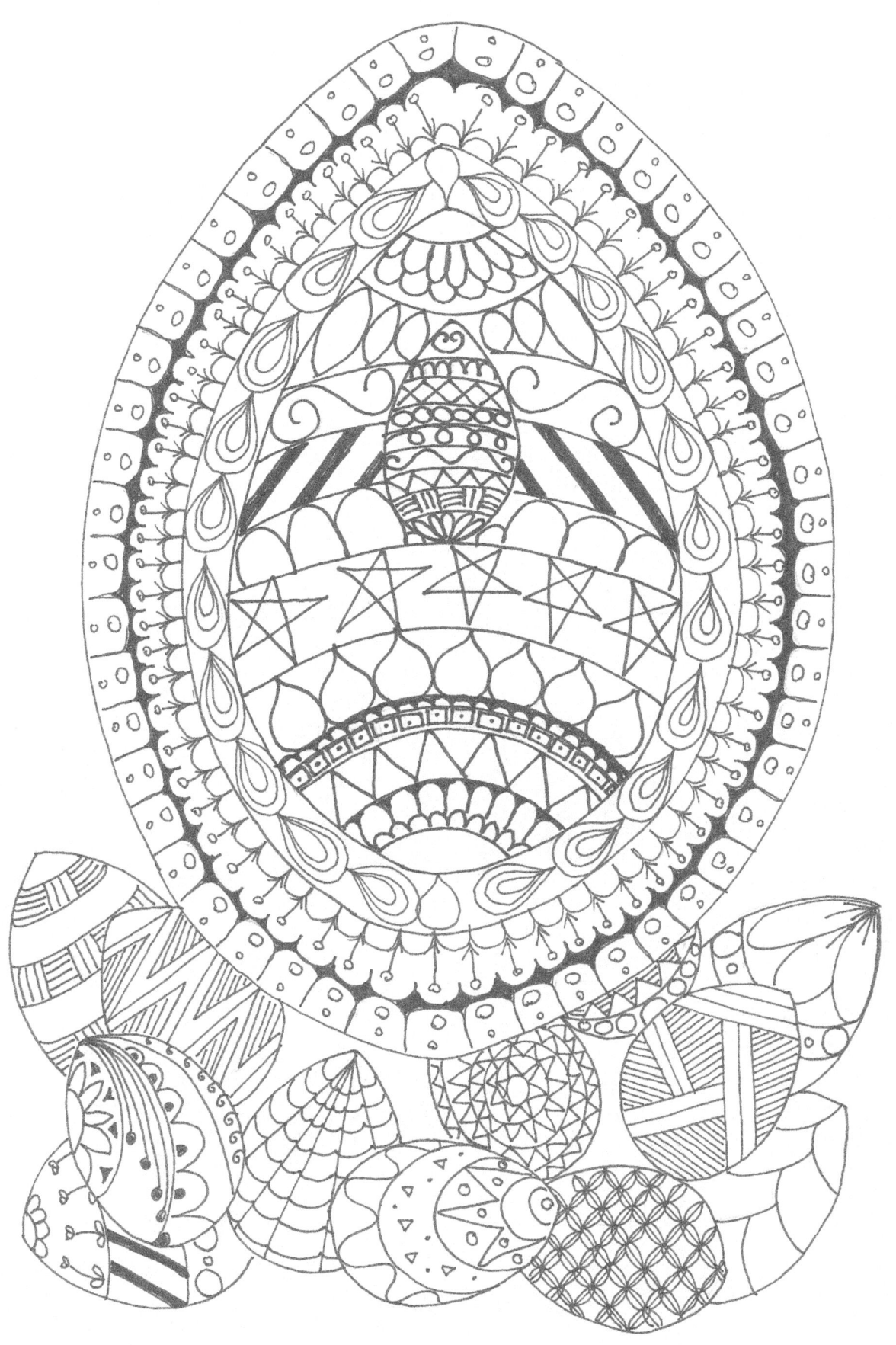

Believe you can and you are half way there.

    Theodore Roosevelt.

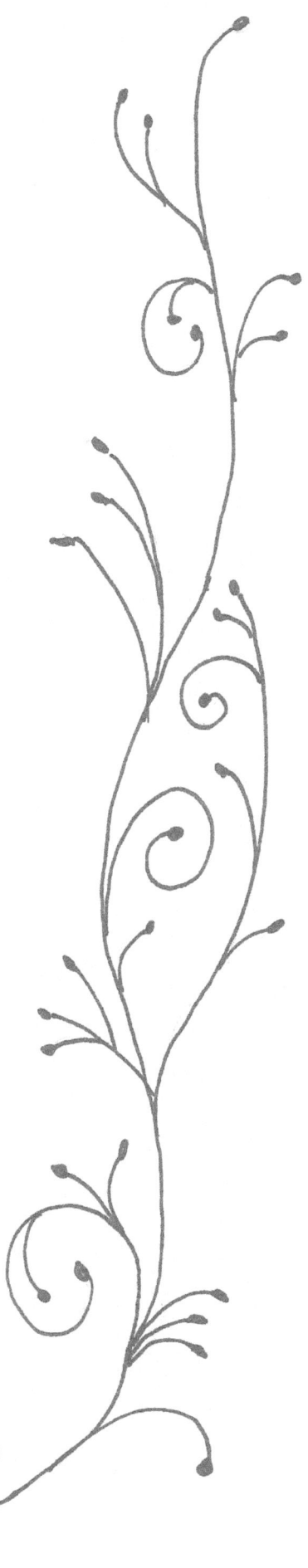

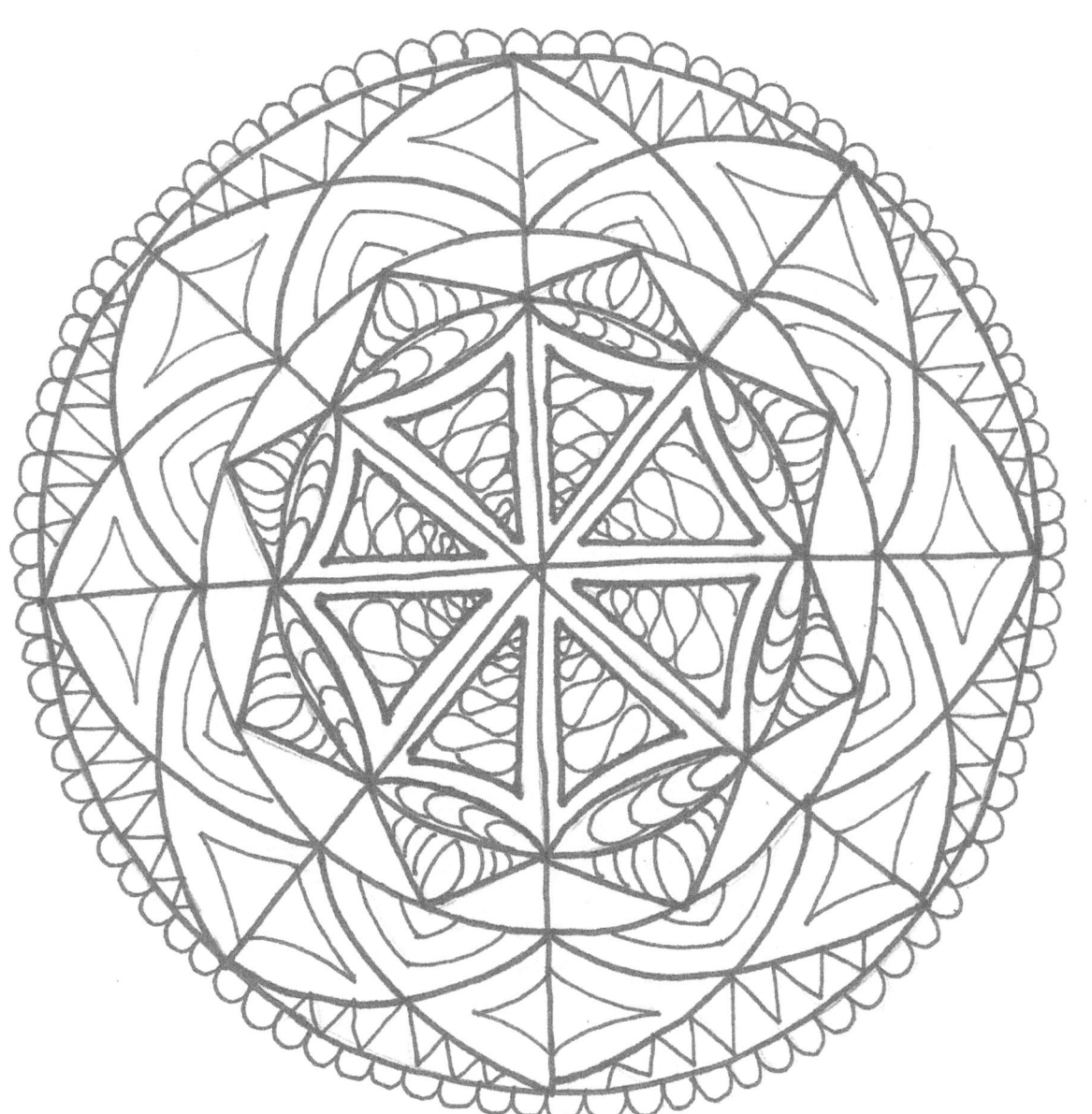

Turn your face
to the sun and
the shadows fall
behind you.

     Anon.

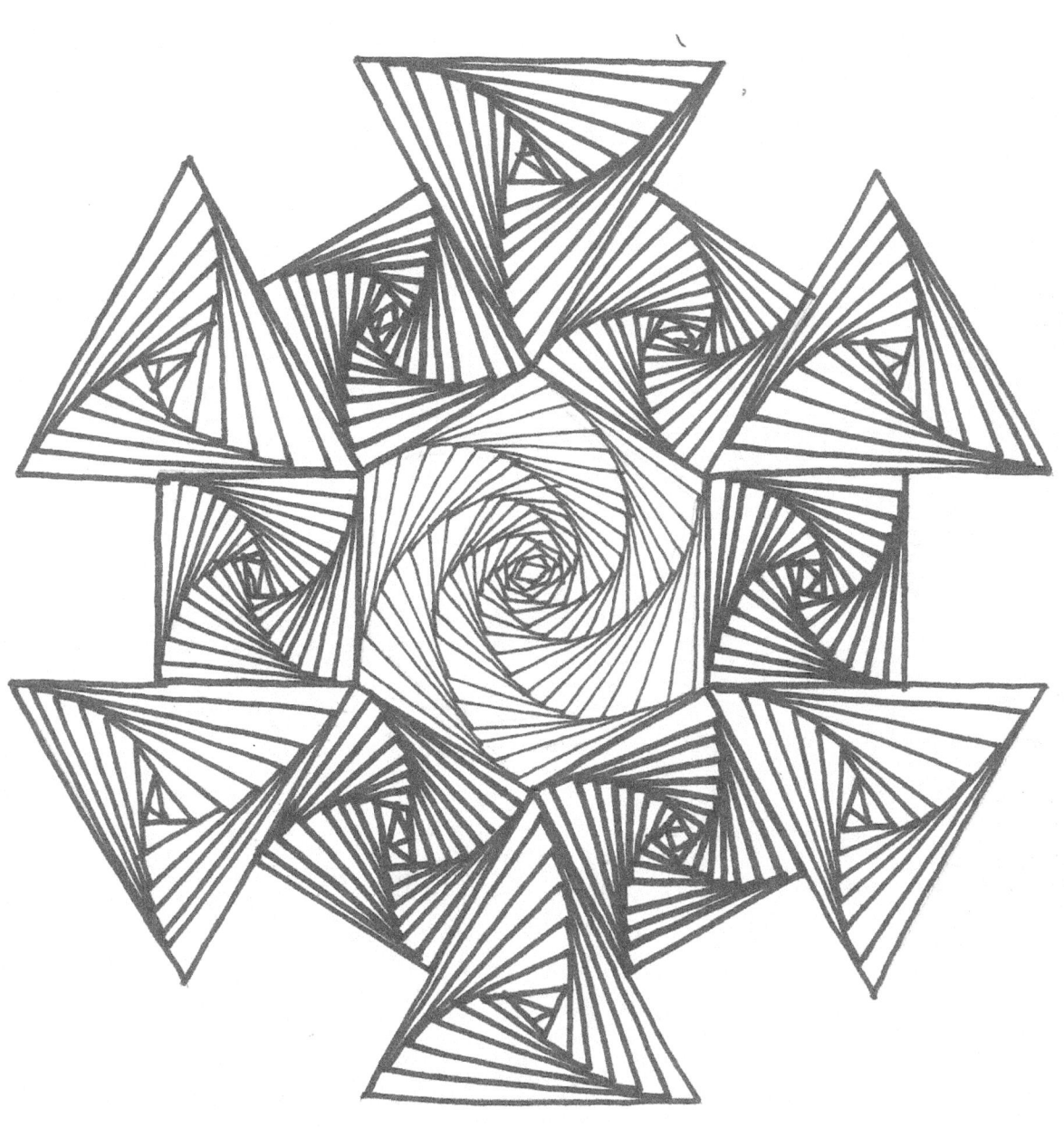

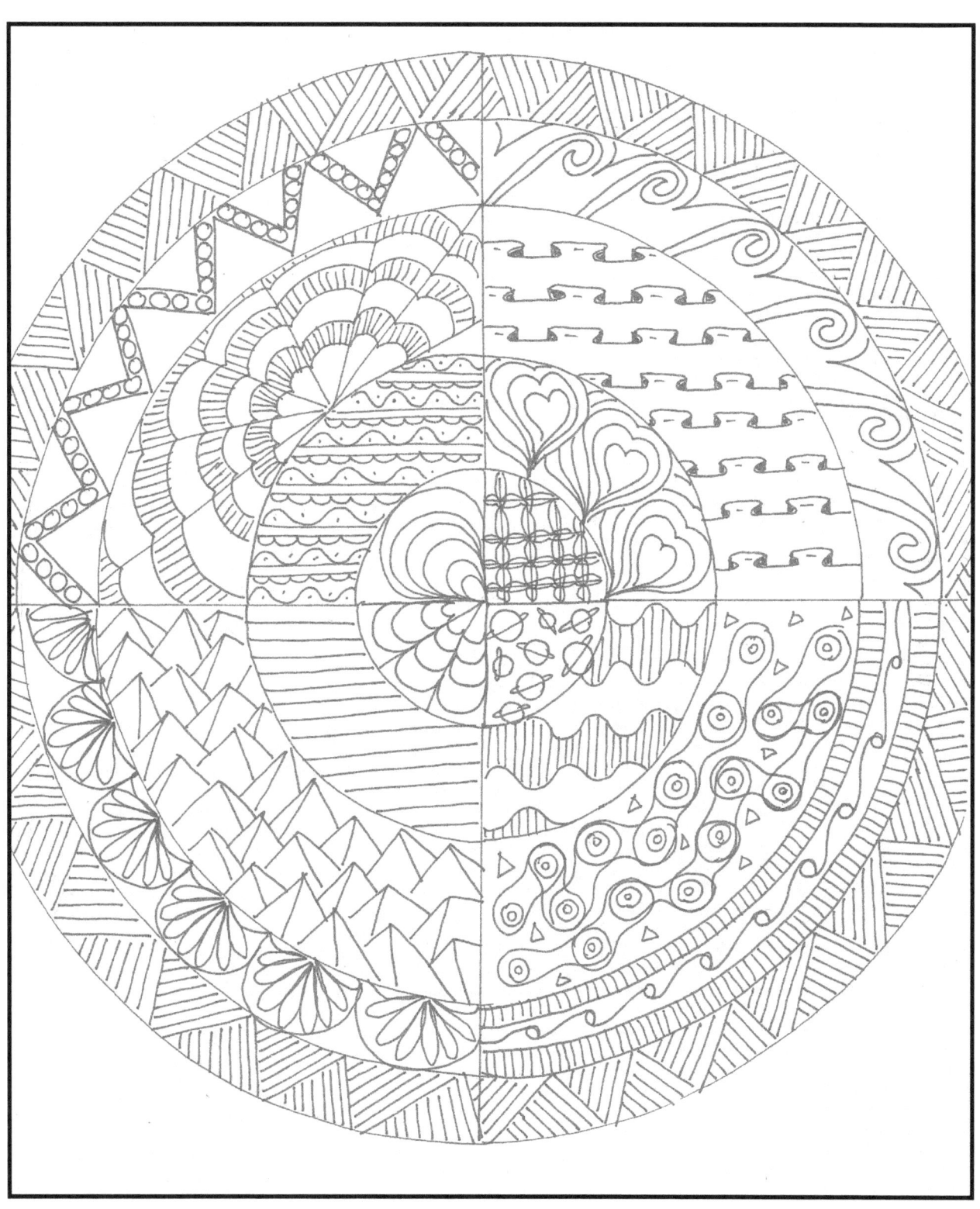

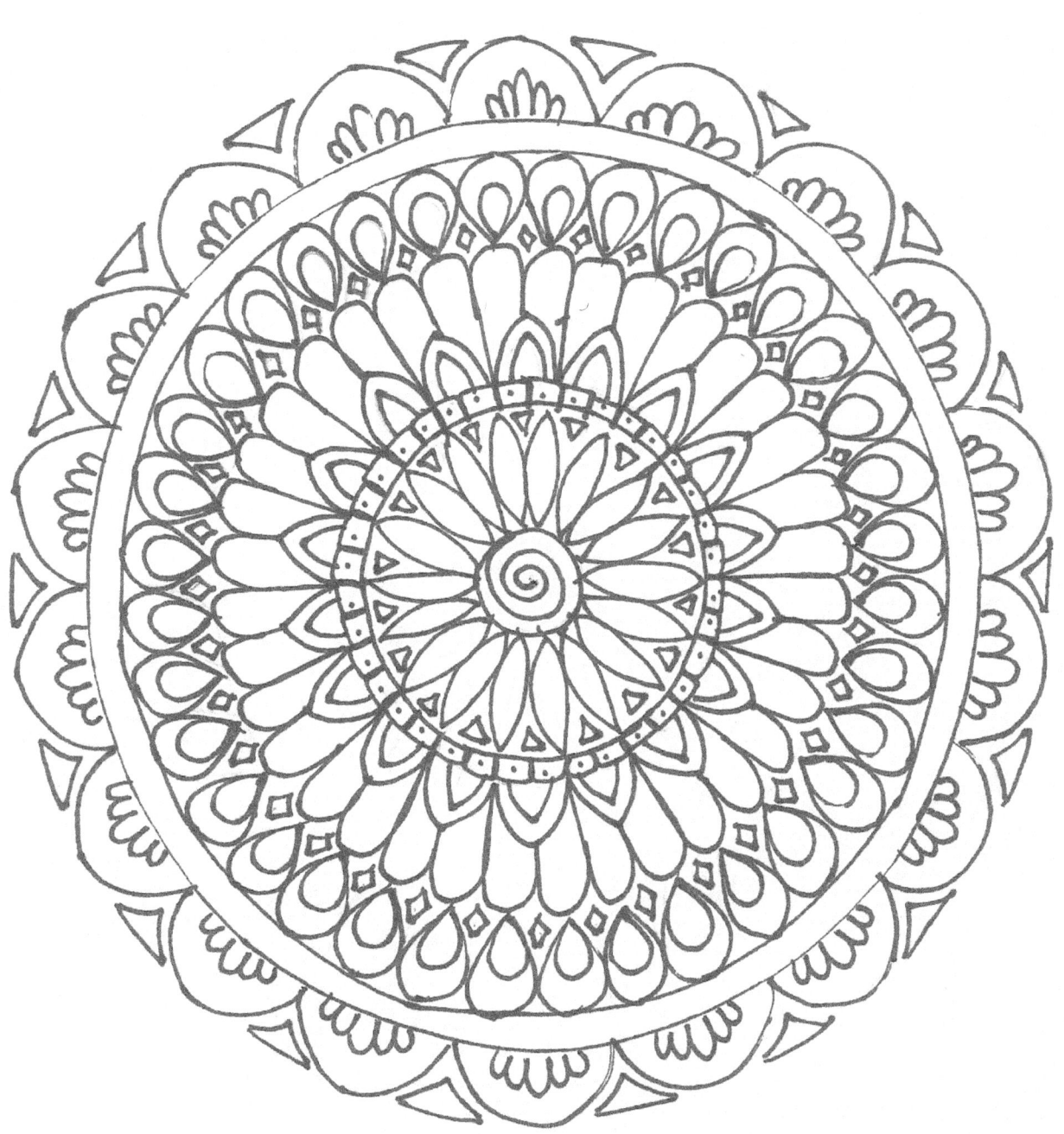

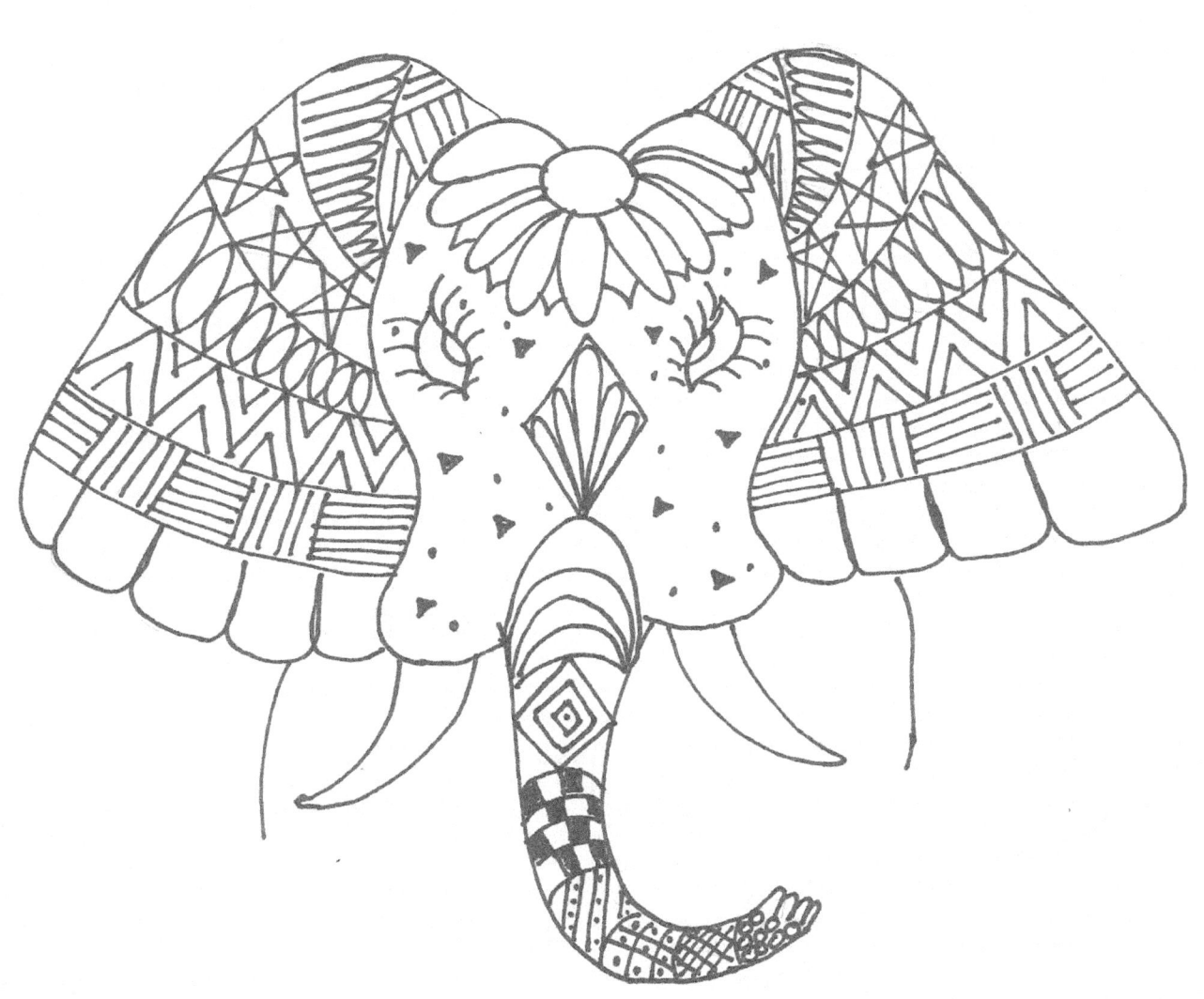

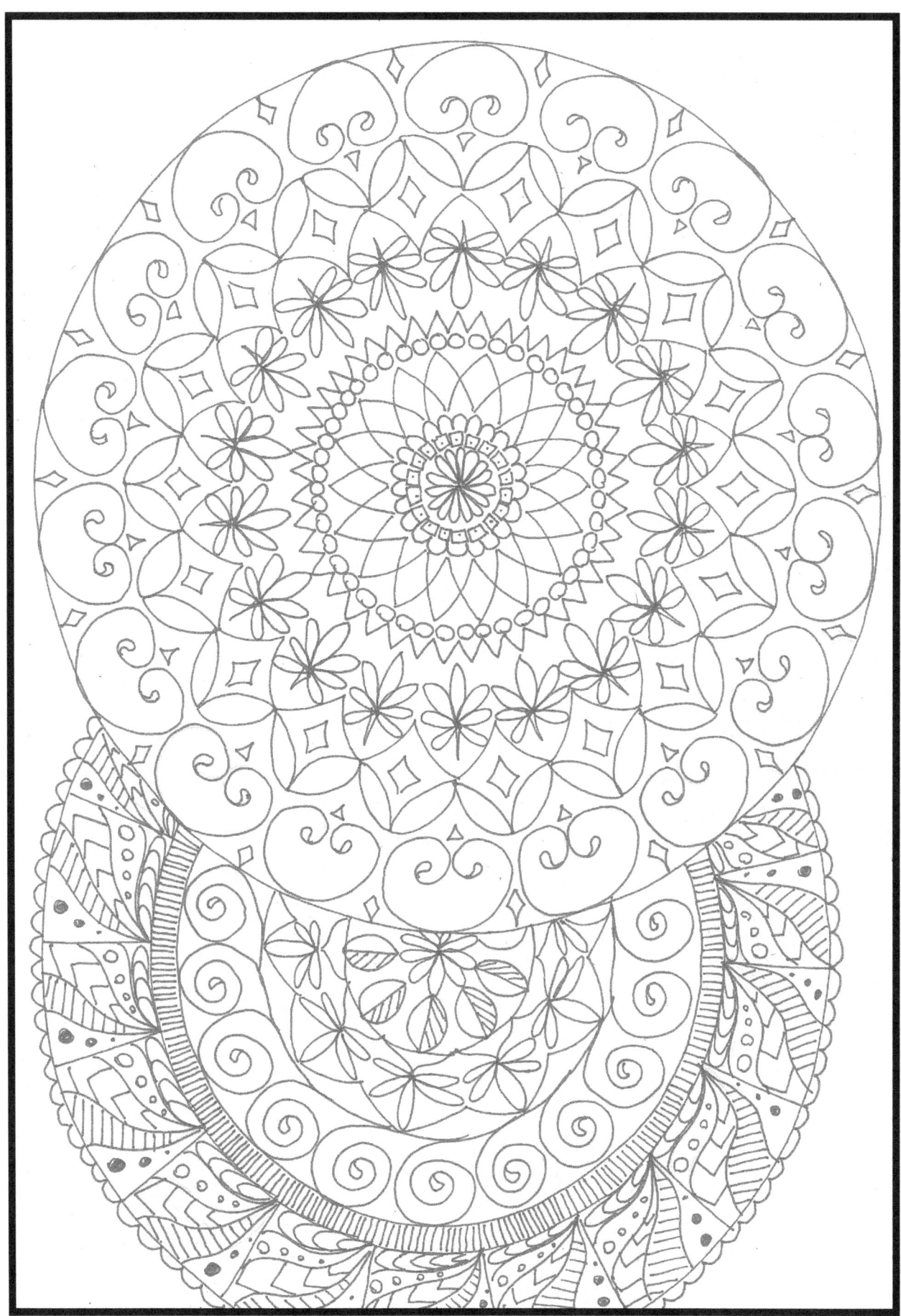

Climb that mountain.

Anon.

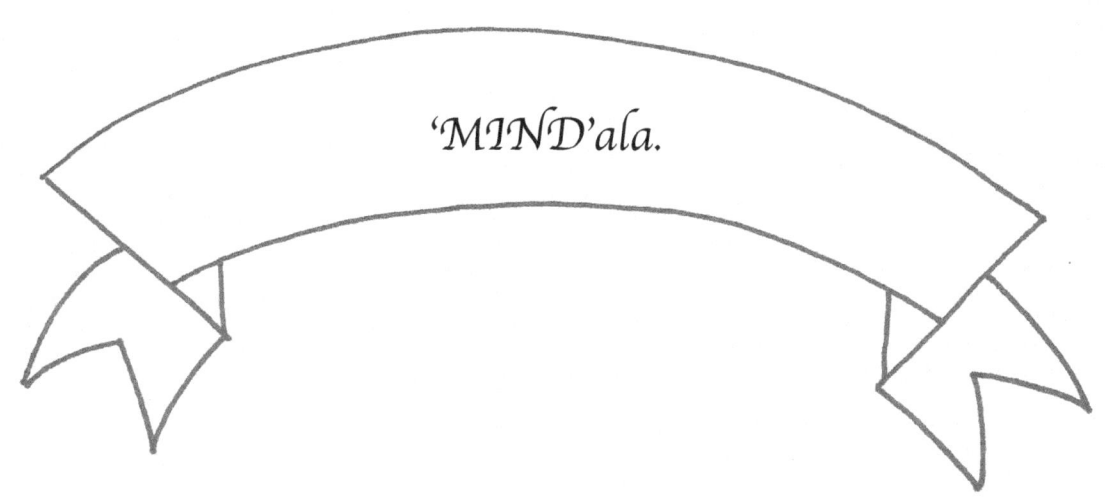
'MIND'ala.

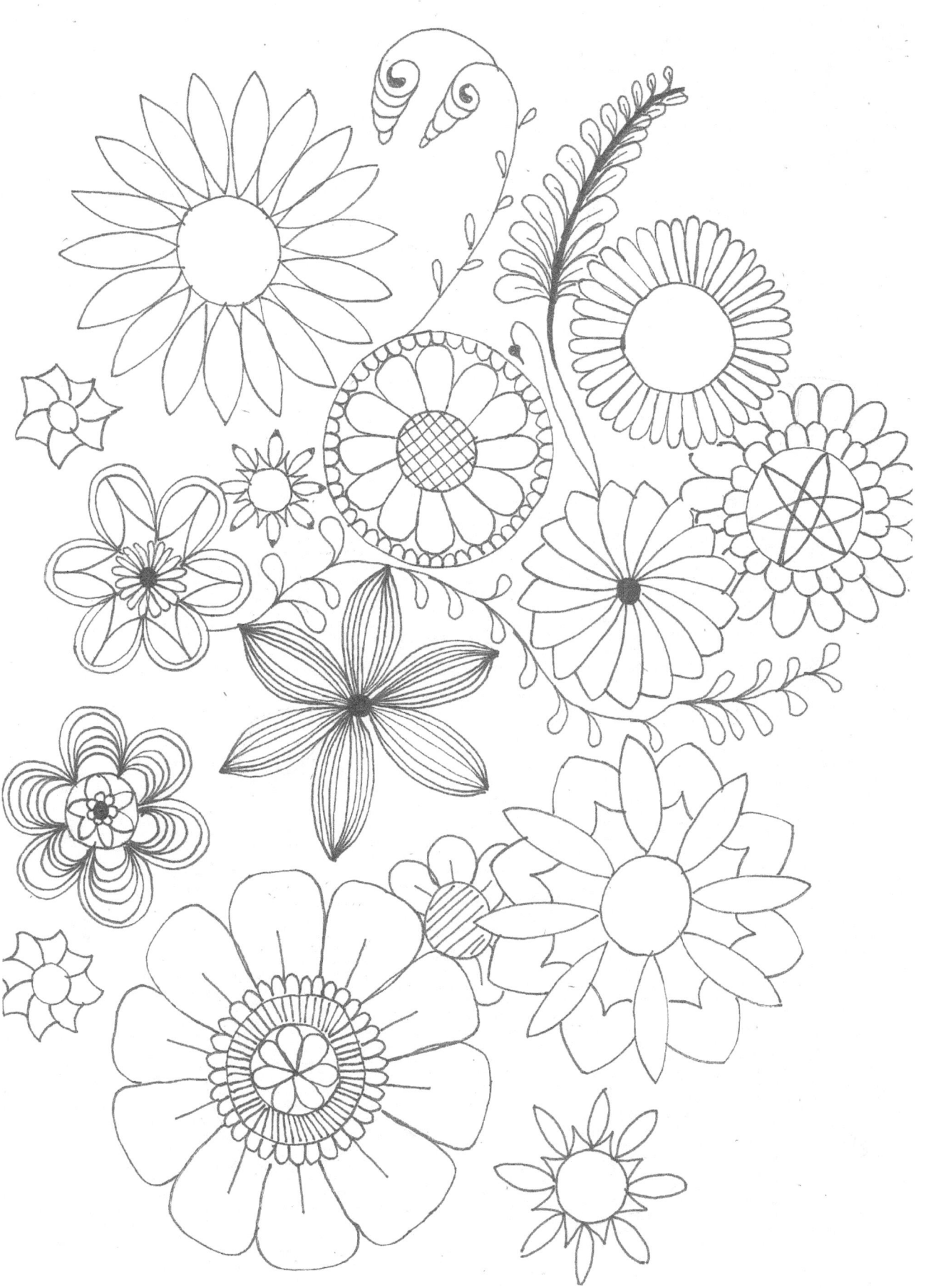

Be like a pineapple, stand tall, wear a crown and be sweet on the inside.

                Anon.

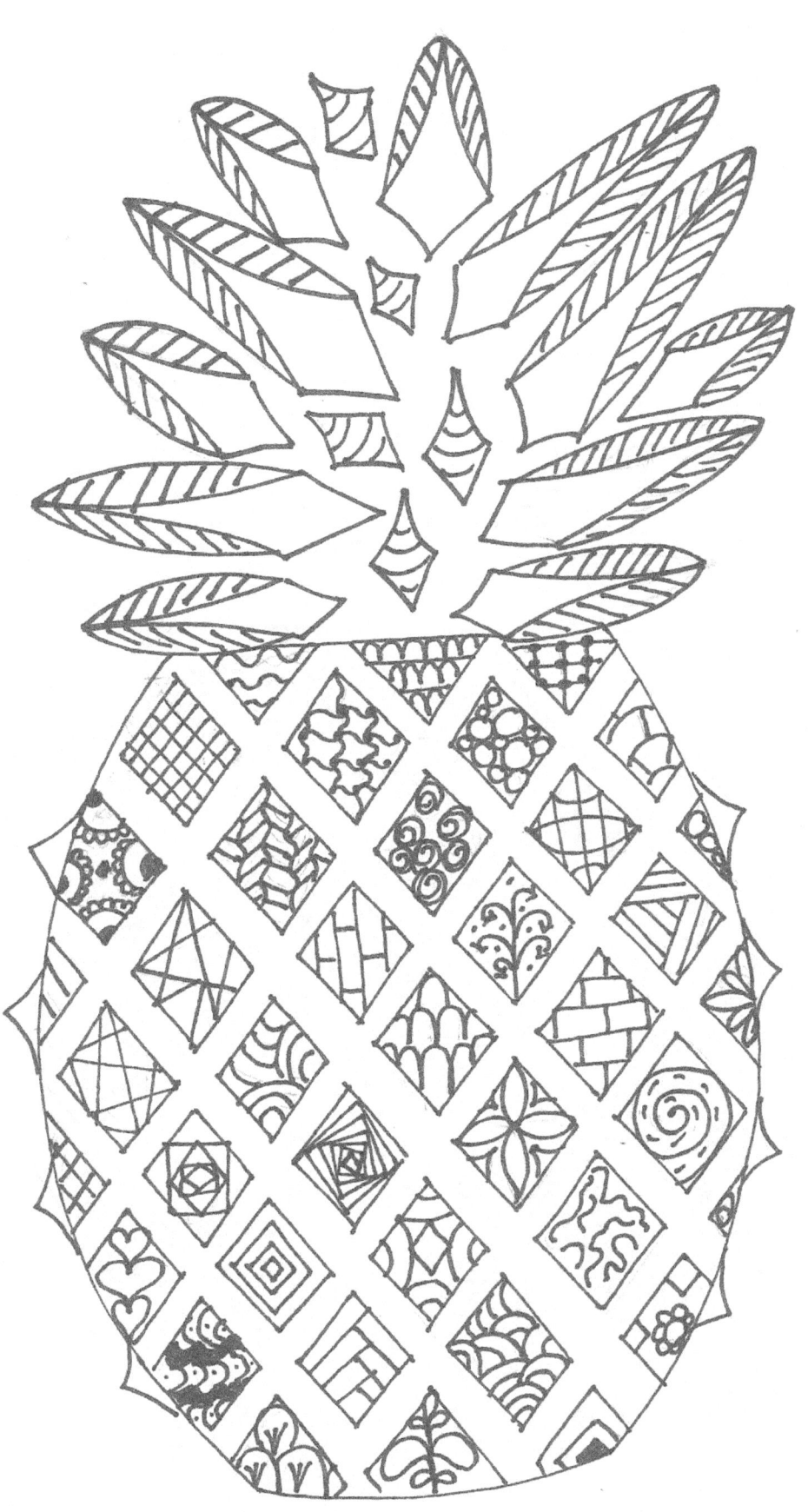

Enjoy life, this is not a rehearsal.

        Anon.

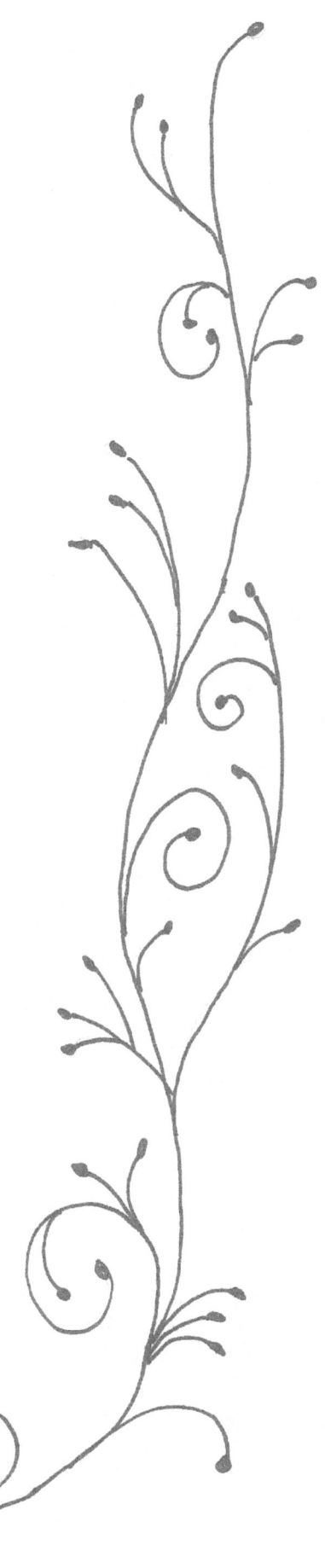

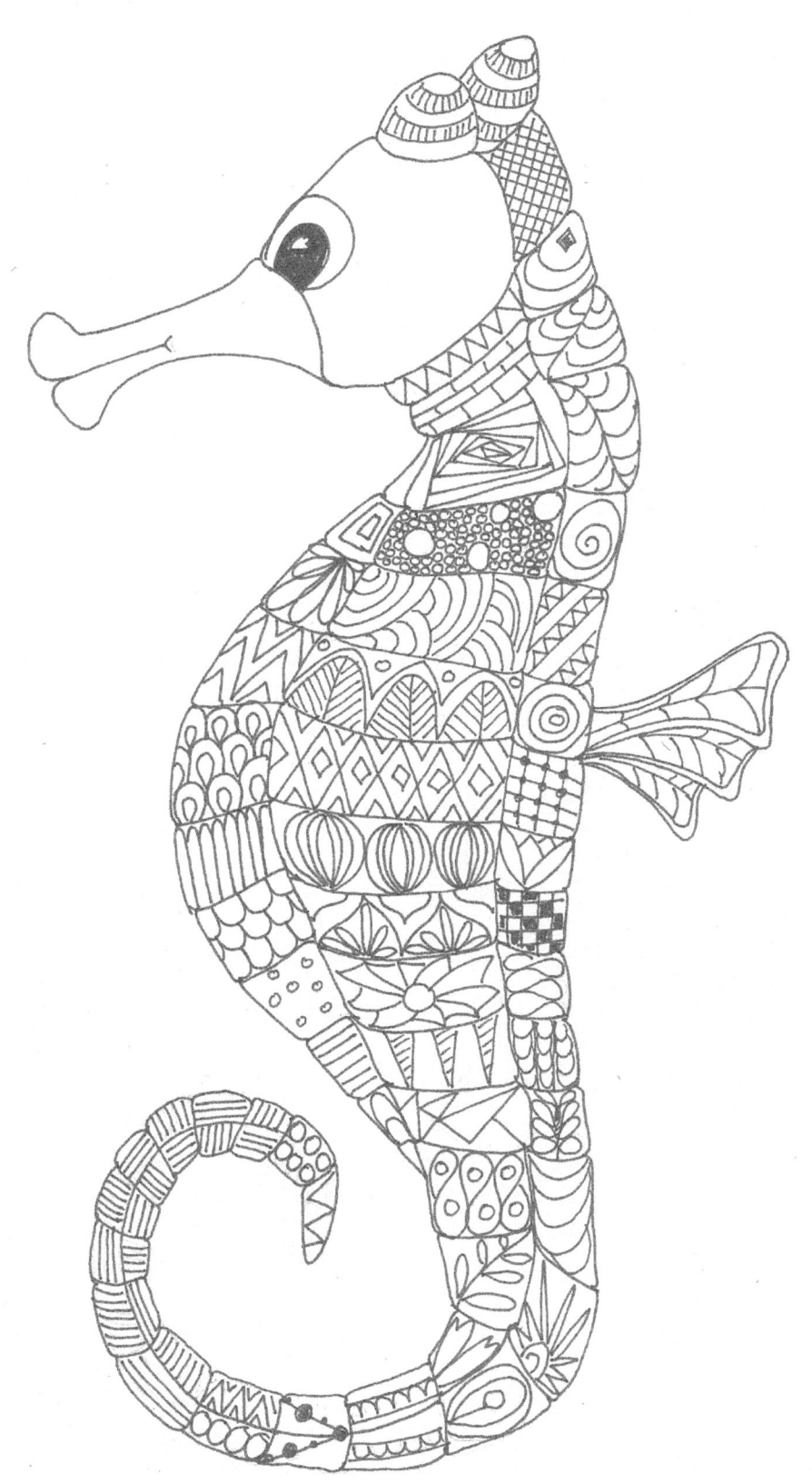

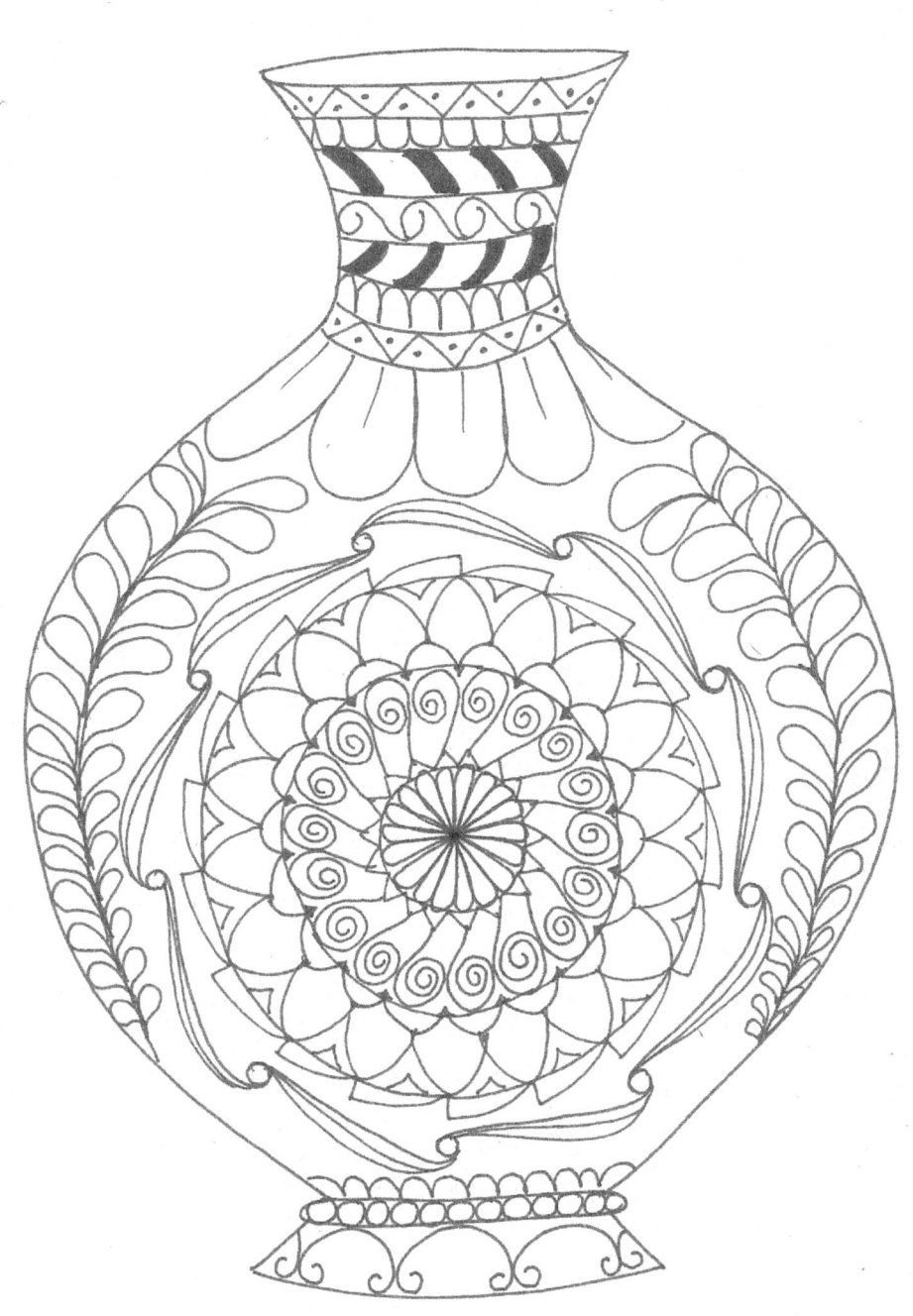

I want to be like a caterpillar; eat a lot, sleep for a while and wake up beautiful.

     Anon.

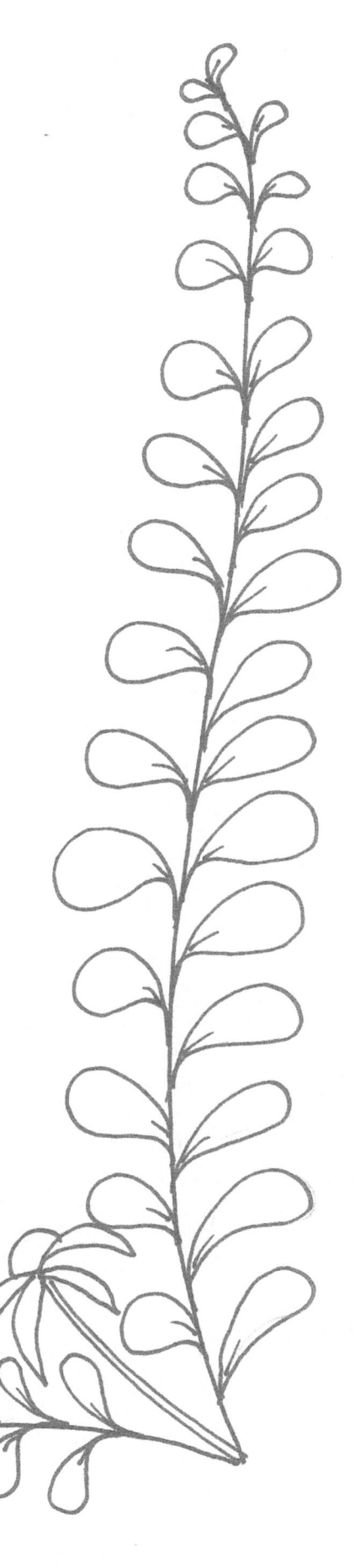

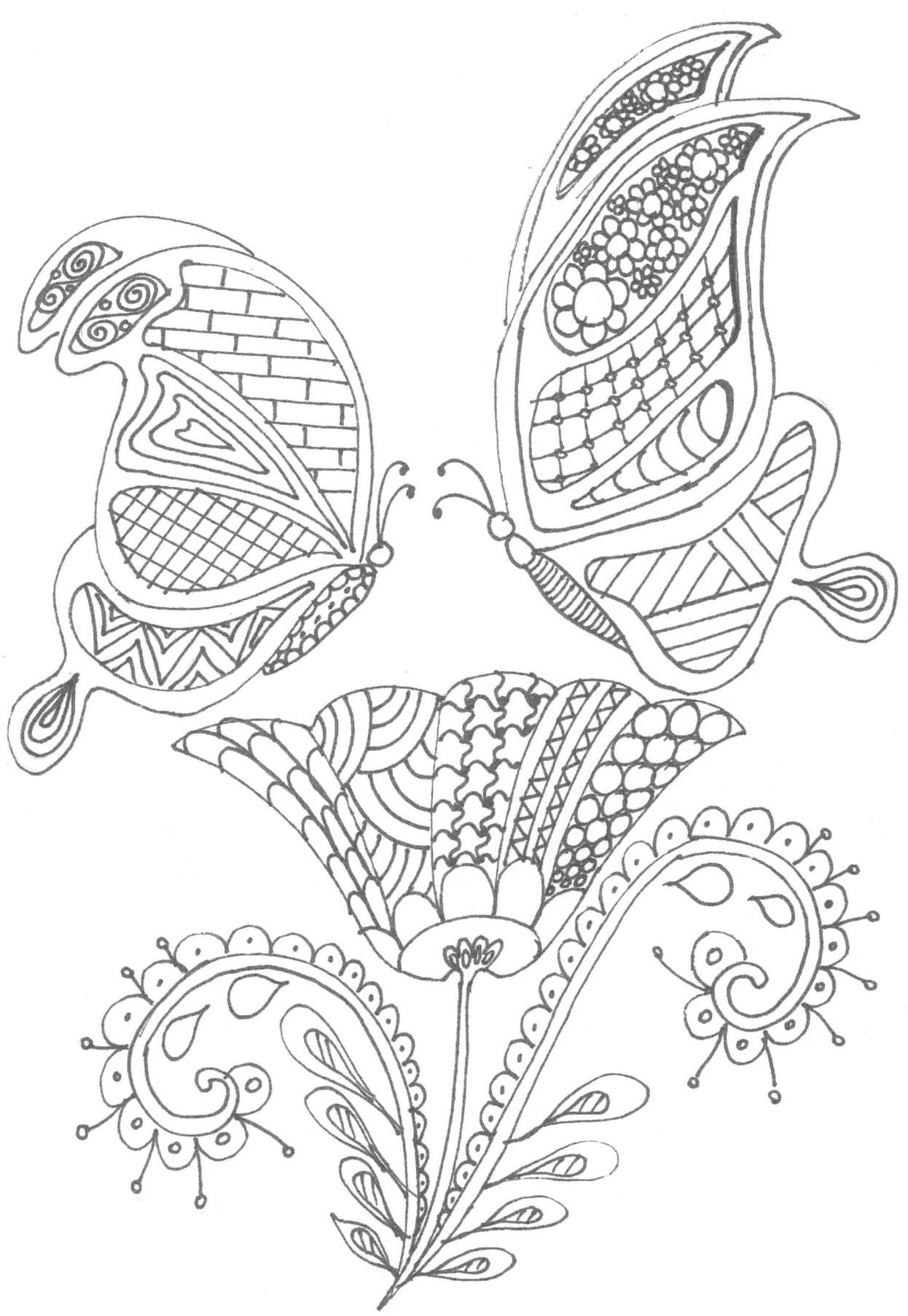

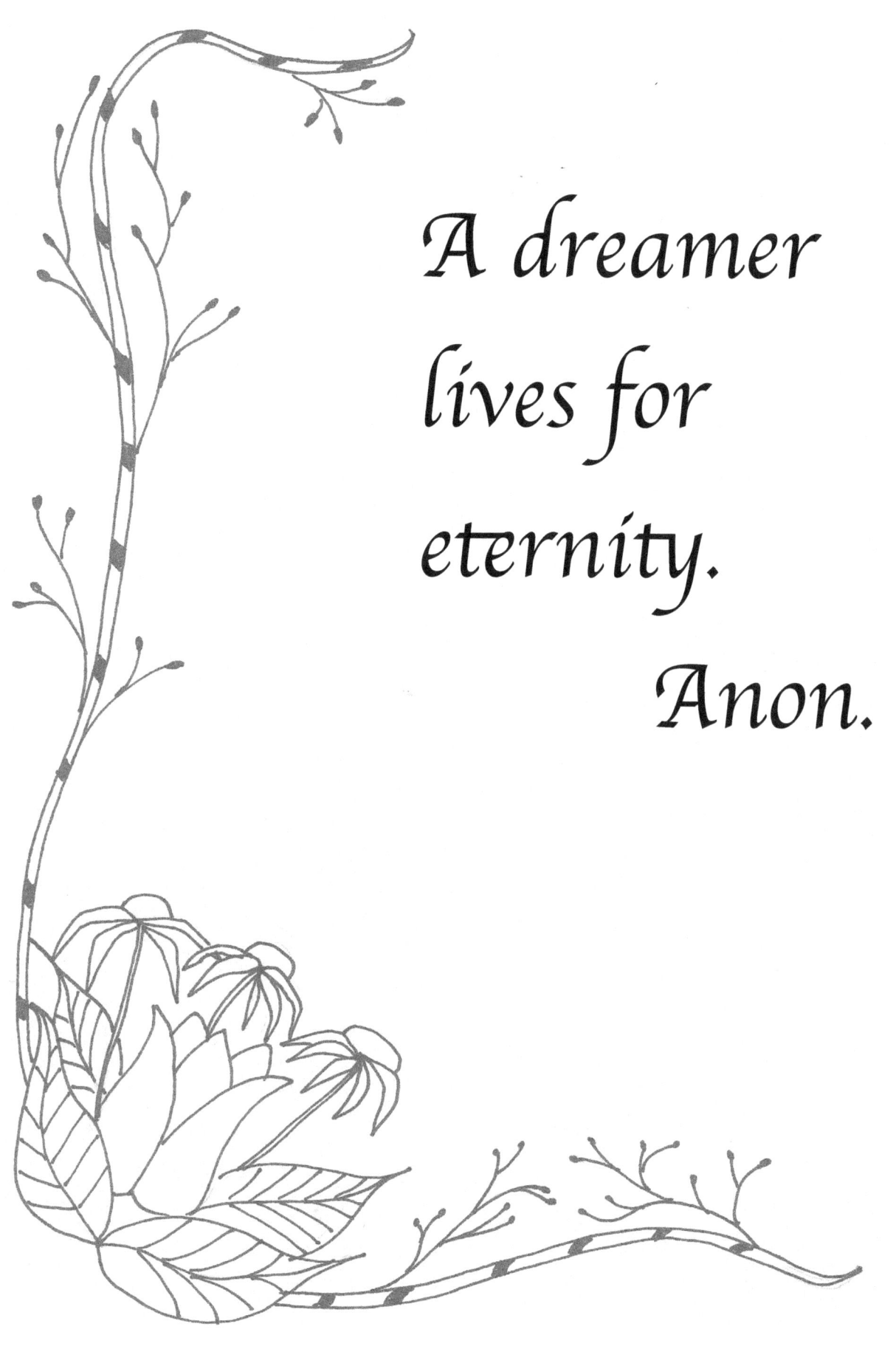

A dreamer lives for eternity.

Anon.

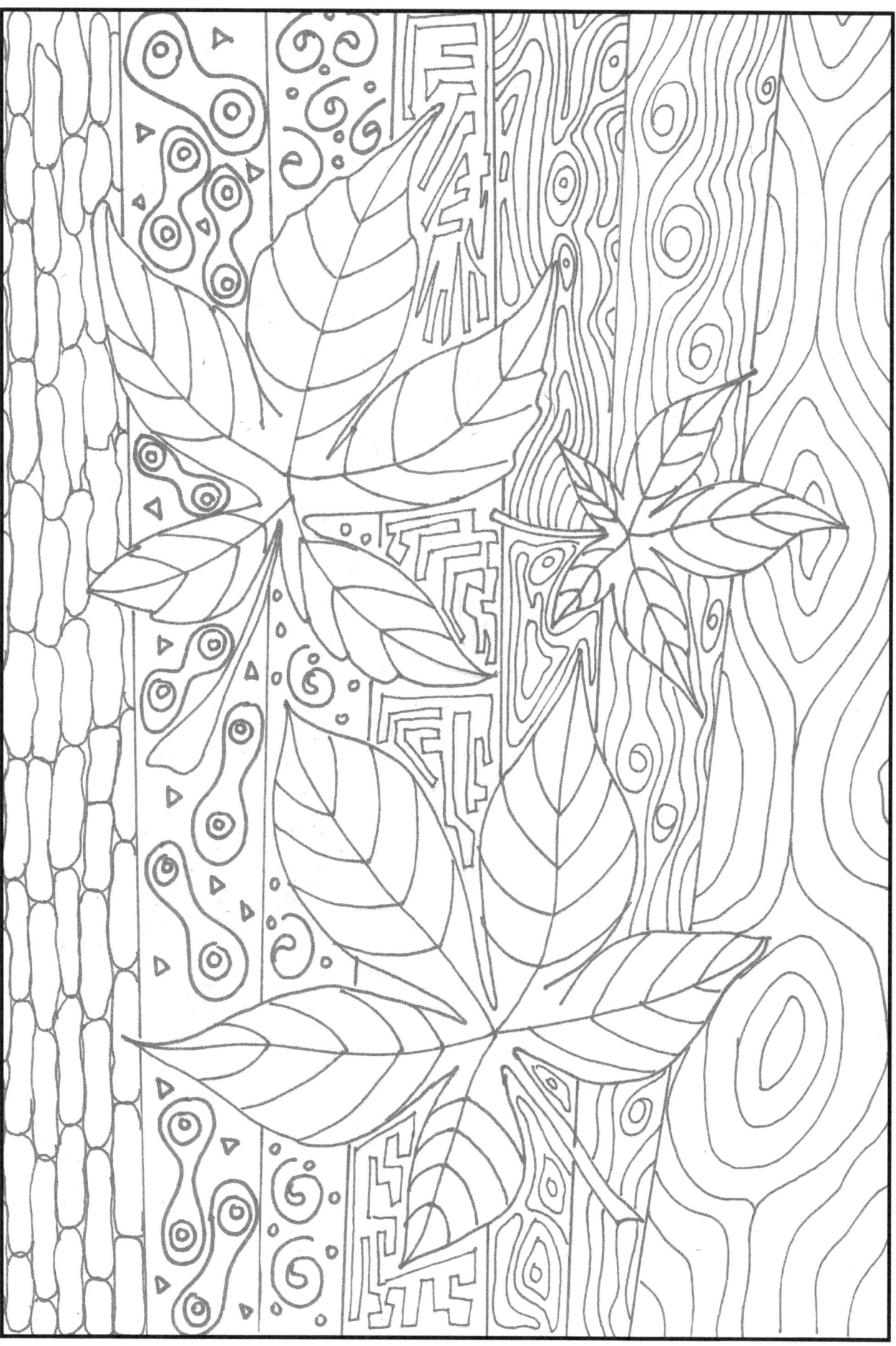

If you never try, you will never know.

                    Anon.

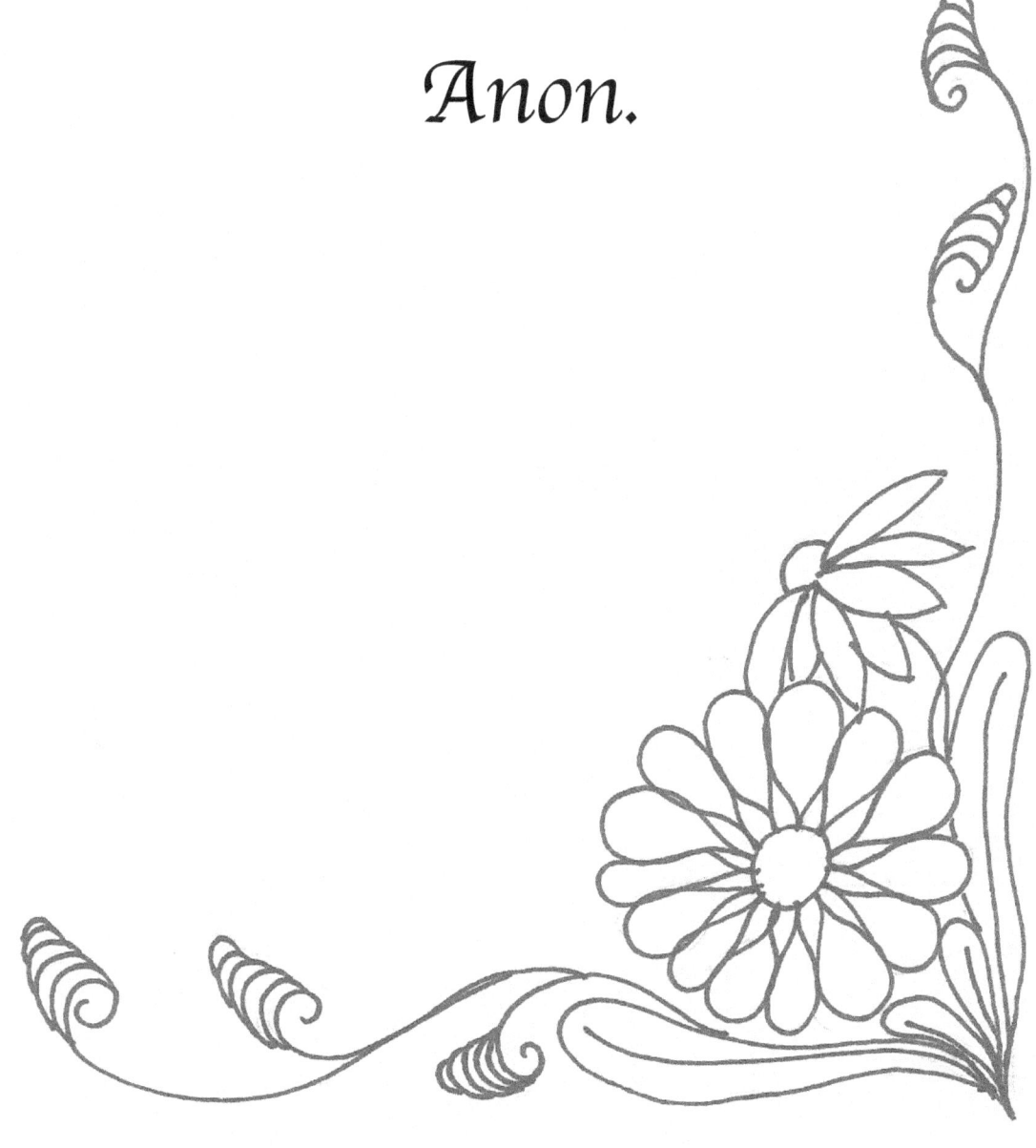

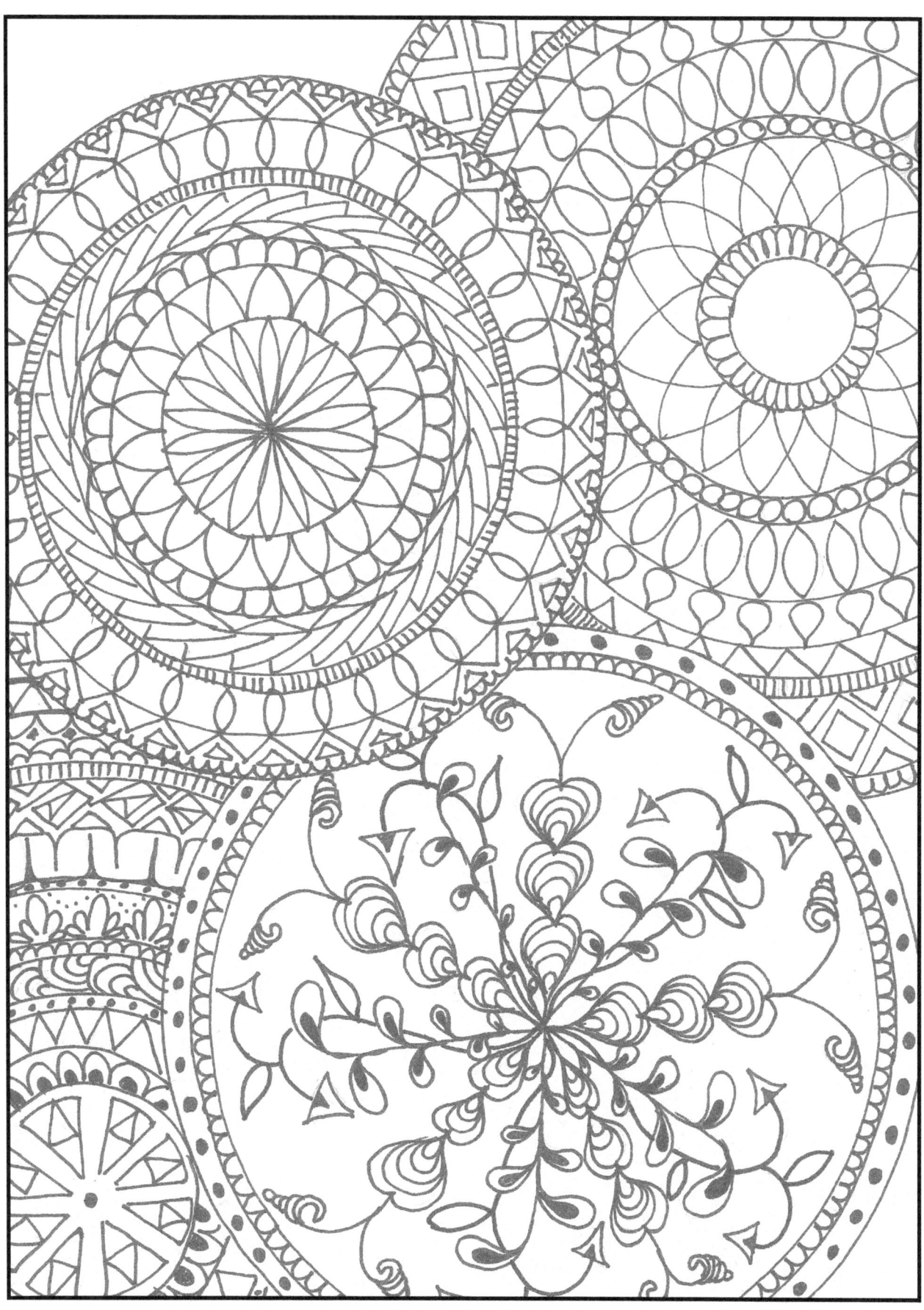

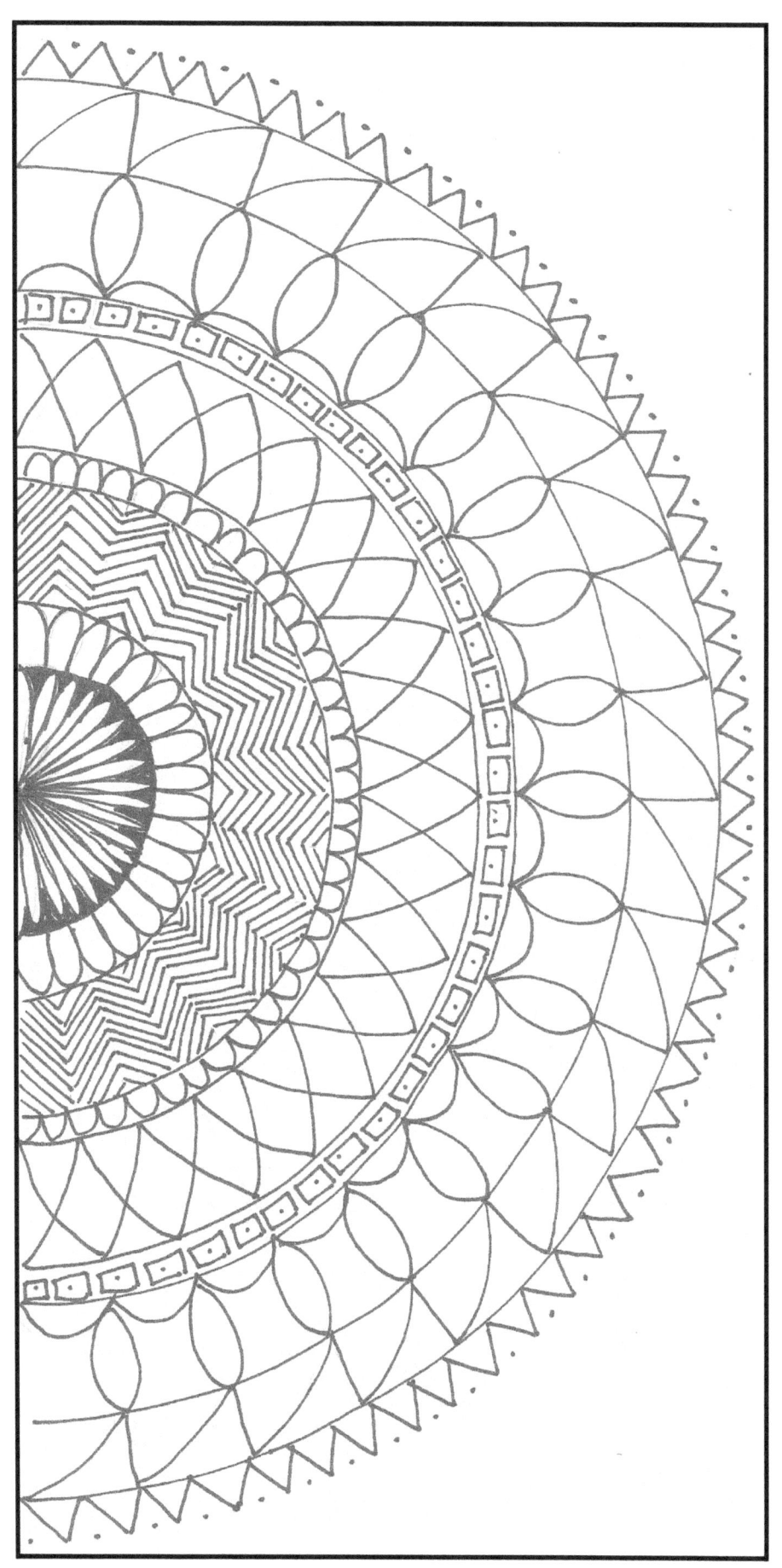

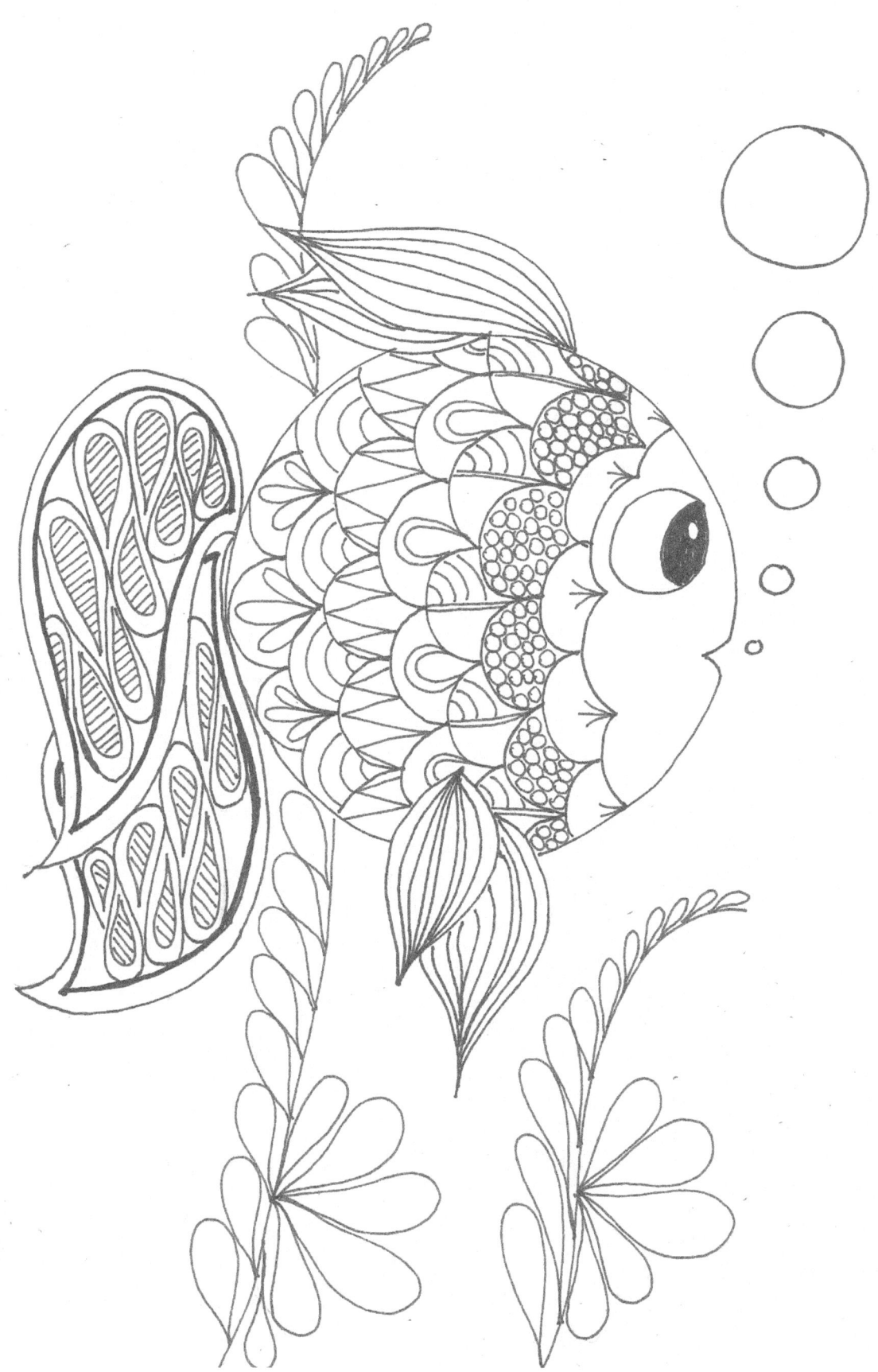

It's all about finding the calm in the chaos.

　　　　Donna Karen.

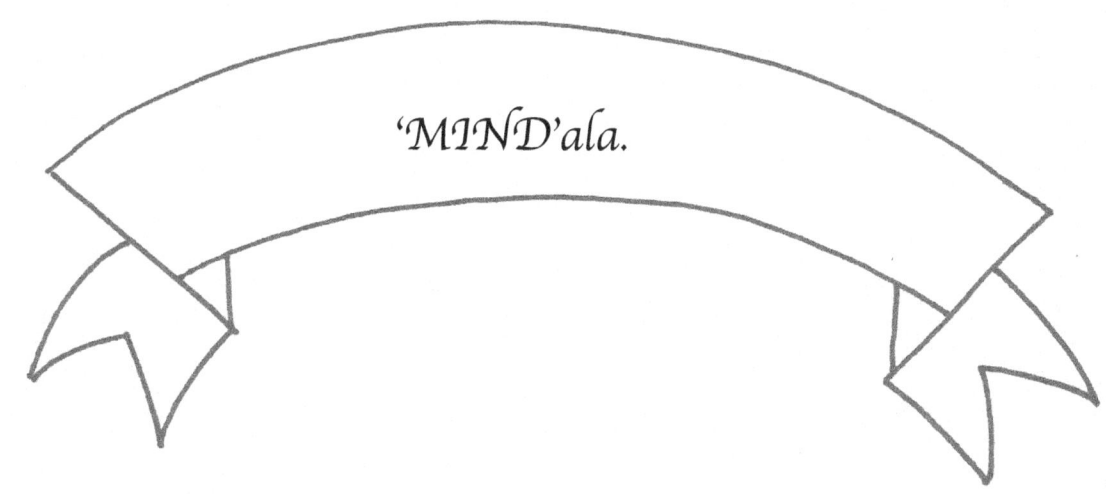
'MIND'ala.

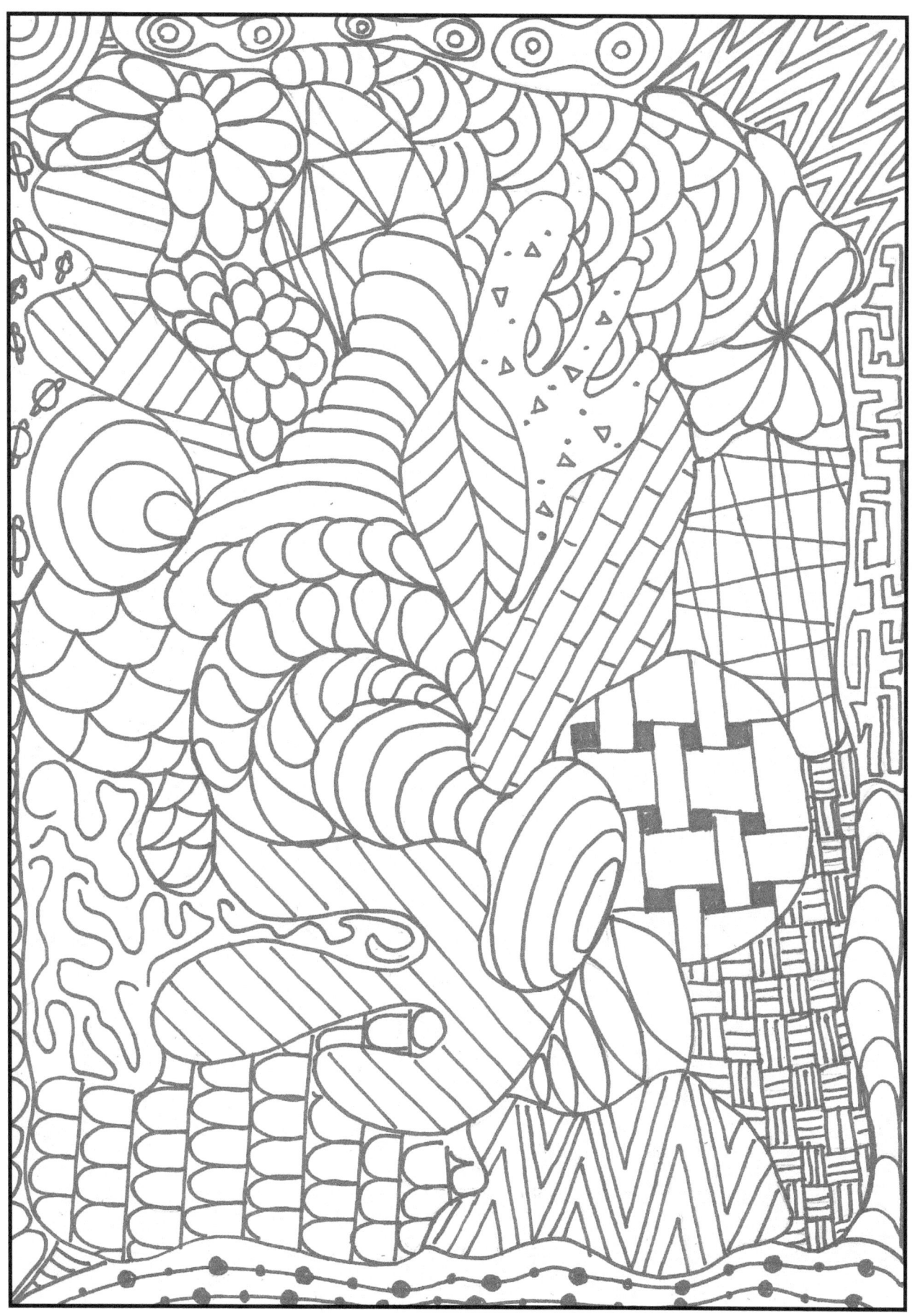

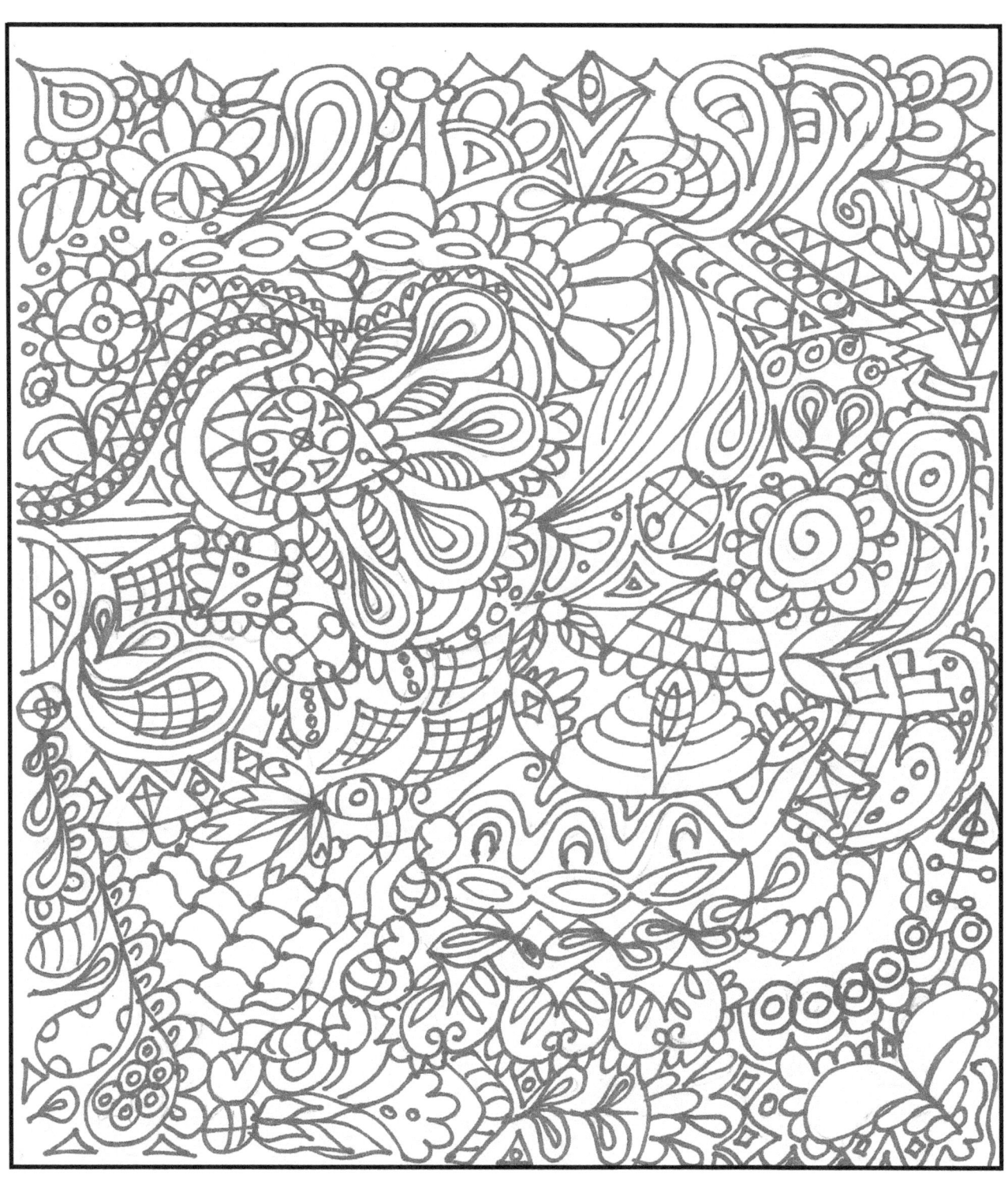

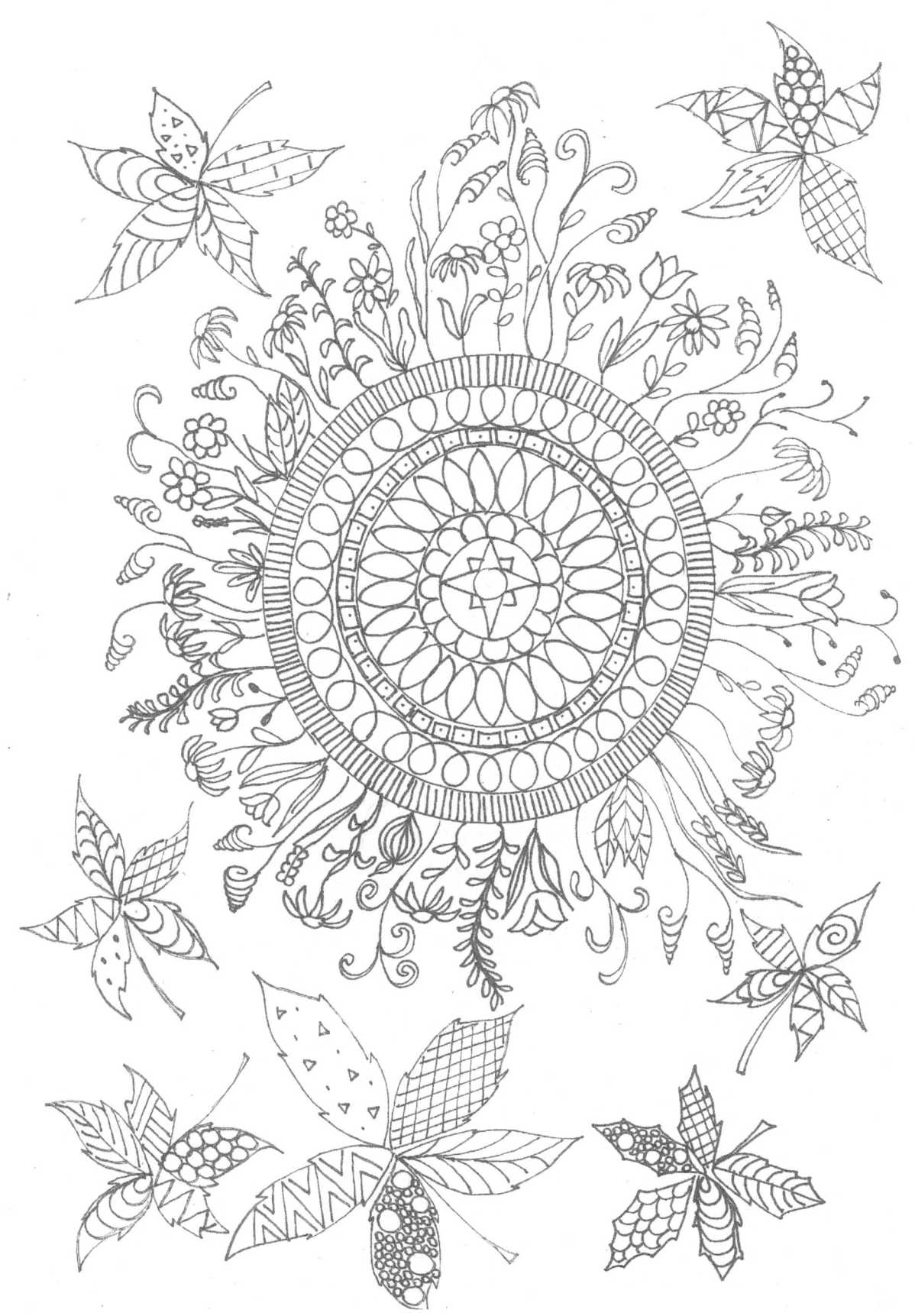

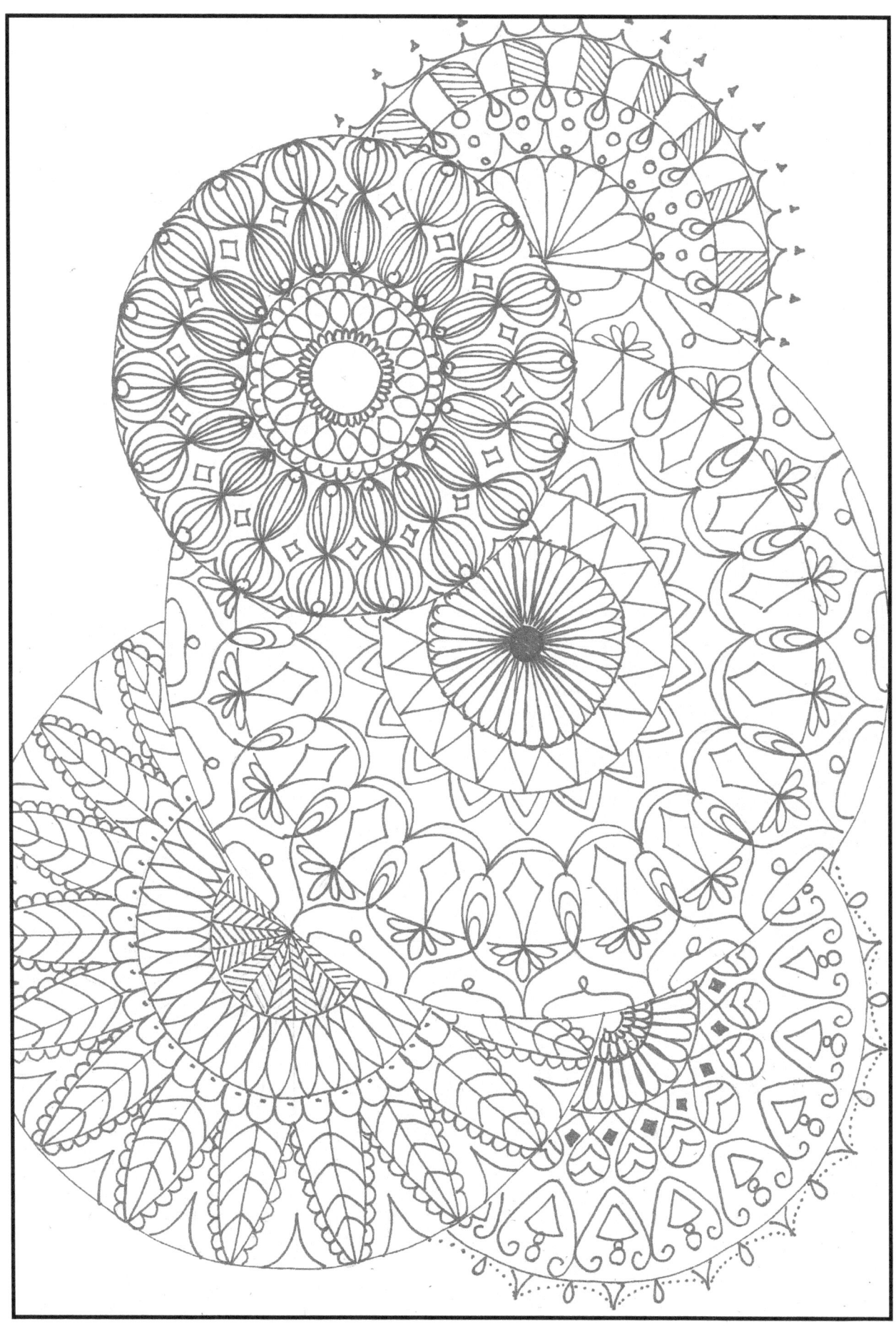

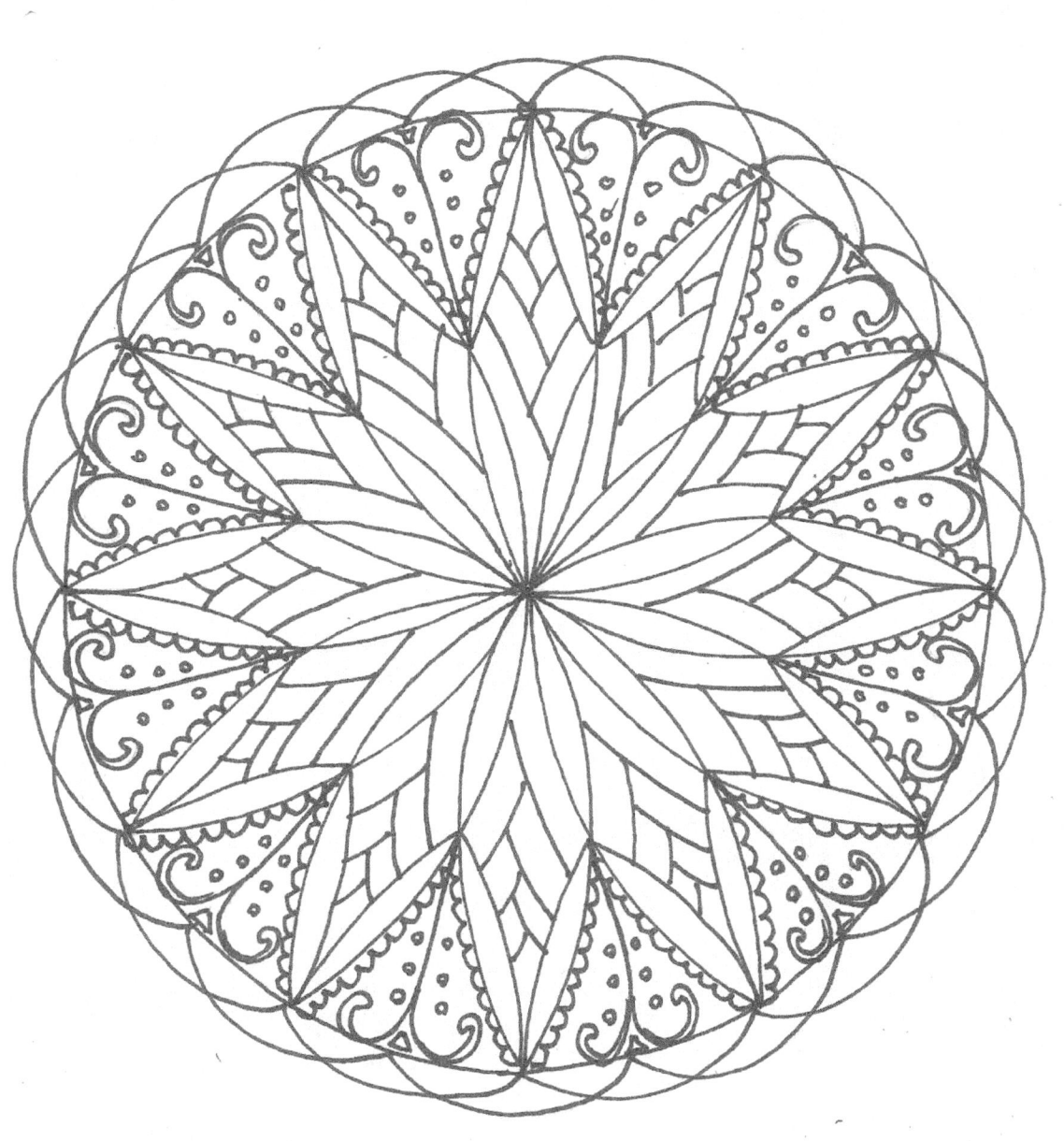

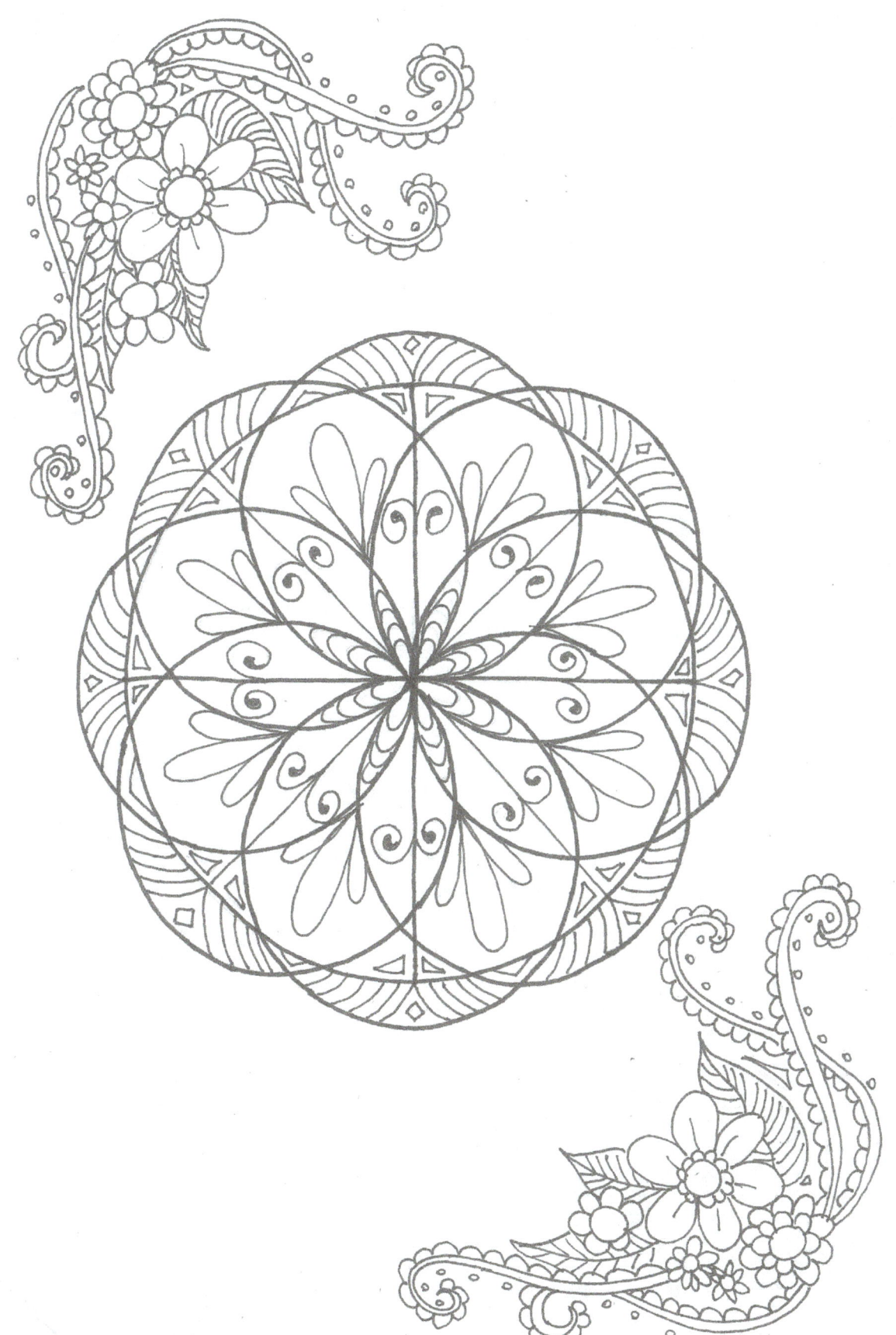

www.ingramcontent.com/pod-product-compliance
Lightning Source LLC
Chambersburg PA
CBHW082342220526
45470CB00008B/2608